SMART MASTERMIND

Smart Working & Remote Working

-

Psychology of Work and Organizations for Virtual Teams, Collaborative Networks and Mastermind Groups

EDOARDO
ZELONI MAGELLI

© Copyright 2021 Edoardo Zeloni Magelli - All right reserved.

ISBN: 978-1-80154-317-0 - December 2021 - Original Version: Smart Mastermind: Smart Working & Remote Working – Psicologia del Lavoro e delle Organizzazioni per Team Virtuali, Reti Collaborative e Gruppi Mastermind

Author: Psychologist, Businessman and Consultant. Edoardo Zeloni Magelli, born in Prato in 1984. In 2010, soon after graduating in Psychology of Work and Organizations, he launched his first startup. As a Businessman he is CEO of Zeloni Corporation, a training company specialising in Business Applied Mental Sciences. His company is a reference point for anyone who wants to realize an idea or a project. As a scientist of the mind he is the father of Primordial Psychology and helps people to empower their minds in the shortest possible time. A music and sport-lover.

UPGRADE YOUR MIND → zelonimagelli.com

UPGRADE YOUR BUSINESS → zeloni.eu

The content contained within this book may not be reproduced, duplicated or transmitted without direct written permission from the author.

Under no circumstances will any blame or legal responsibility be held against the author, for any damages, reparation, or monetary loss due to the information contained within this book. Either directly or indirectly.

Legal Notice: This book is copyright protected. This book is only for personal use. You cannot amend, distribute, sell, use, quote or paraphrase any part, or the content within this book, without the consent of the author or publisher.

Disclaimer Notice: Please note the information contained within this document is for educational and entertainment purposes only. All effort has been executed to present accurate, up to date, and reliable, complete information. No warranties of any kind are declared or implied. Readers acknowledge that the author is not engaging in the rendering of legal, financial, medical or professional advice. The content within this book has been derived from various sources. Please consult a licensed professional before attempting any techniques outlined in this book.

By reading this document, the reader agrees that under no circumstances is the author responsible for any losses, direct or indirect, which are incurred as a result of the use of information contained within this document, including, but not limited to, — errors, omissions, or inaccuracies.

CONTENTS

Introduction 7
   Harmony and Balance between Online and Offline 9
   Give Your Business a Boost 12

1. Smart Working 13
   Benefits of Smart Working 15
      Increases Productivity 15
      Management Improvement 16
      The Environment 16
   Disadvantages of Smart Working 17
      Finances 17
      Decreased Productivity 17
      Isolation 18
      Hyperconnection, Workaholism and Burnout
         Syndrome 18
   Smart Working Tips 21

2. Remote Working 29
   Benefits of Remote Working 30
      Flexibility and Freedom 30

    Mental Health Improvement...................................31
    Reduced Costs..31
    Work From Anywhere..32
    Increase in Productivity...34

Disadvantages of Remote Working.................................34

    Employee Disconnect...34
    Unbalanced Work/Life..35
    Distractions..35
    Disrupted Work Culture..36

Remote Working Tips...36

    How to Take Effective Breaks (and Be More Productive)..38

How to Increase Productivity..41

    Single-Handing..43
    Increase Concentration..43
    Email Management..47
    Learn to Manage Distractions..............................54
    The Empowering Environment............................56

3. The Importance of Collaboration............................67

Benefits of Collaboration...70
    Collaboration Tips..72
Harnessing the Web for International Collaboration....75

  Types of Collaboration..75
  How to Grow and Interact with Network
    Collaboration..86
  How to Use Smart and Remote Working with
    Network Collaboration...92
  The Traps of Virtual Reality..99

4. The Mastermind Group..103

  The Master Mind...104
    The Chemistry of the Mind.......................................105
    The Perfect Harmony...108
    Mastermind Groups..111
  How to Create a Mastermind Group............................116
  Benefits of a Mastermind Group..................................119
  The Virtual Mastermind Group....................................121
    Advantages and Disadvantages of a Virtual
      Mastermind Group..121

5. Virtual Teams...123

  How to Create a Virtual Team......................................123
    Advantages and Disadvantages of Virtual Teams...134
  How to Effectively Manage and Optimize Performance
    of a Virtual Team...135
    Increase Collaboration Skills......................................137

    Effective Habits for Teams..140

    Virtues of Virtual Teams..143

    Tips on Virtual Teams..144

Conclusion...149

    The Limits Are Only in Your Mind............................150

Bibliographical References..153

Introduction

Whether we like it or not, the future of business will be conducted online, as long as the global Internet infrastructure works. Using data from a FlexJobs study, remote working has exploded in the last two decades growing 159% from 2005 to 2017 (Bayern, 2019). With workplace disruptions caused by the changes in the last few years, the number of remote workers worldwide nearly tripled. Using the United States as an example, at the peak, 44% of the American population worked remotely full time, in comparison to 17% pre-2019 (Miltz, 2020). While that peak number would go down as restrictions eased, and workers went back into the offices, the ripple effects have been clear: business has changed.

According to a study conducted by Growmotely, 74% of working professionals surveyed, as well as 76% of entrepreneurs, agree that working remotely will be the new normal (Prossack, 2021). Additionally, most people prefer working online. Looking at a some analysis conducted by PMI.it and T-Voice, 80.74% of Italians would like to work remotely at least two days of their week and 76.8% would like to alternate working days between office and home (PMI.it, 2021).

While change can sometimes be frightening, this change (work from home) isn't one to be afraid of. Instead, it should be embraced. Studies have shown that whether you're a working adult, entrepreneur, or business owner, working from home not only lowers costs for everyone but increases productivity. If the people prefer it, it lowers costs, and increases productivity, why wouldn't you want to work online from home? The positives vastly outweigh the negatives.

Whether you're a business owner considering moving your business online, or an employee or entrepreneur preparing for the future, there is a lot to learn about working online.

If you're still unsure about what exactly remote working entails, this book will cover it all. If you want to know how to maximize your effectiveness working online, this book will answer those questions, too. If you're curious about how to collaborate with others, create and manage your virtual teams, and form mastermind groups, you'll find all of your answers here.

Be ahead of the curve and adopt an efficient and effective online business model today.

Harmony and Balance between Online and Offline

Before I proceed, I'd like to clarify something. Although I'm all for remote work and online businesses, I remain an incurable romantic lover of the culture and craft and culinary traditions of the past.

As I write this, I think of the historic shops in cities, the famous "old-fashioned stores" that are disappearing.

I'm referring to the wonderful craft stores where you can find typical and native products of the place, grocery stores and neighborhood retail, the small business, bakeries, pastry shops, greengrocers, milkmen, delicatessens, wine bars, trattorias, taverns, shoemakers, hatters, leather goods, jewelry, blacksmiths' forges and craft workshops.

Now I'm having nostalgic memories, thinking about walks in the historic center of my Prato, but also of the other medieval towns and villages of my Tuscany. If I close my eyes, I can still hear graceful voices in the background coming from those timeless alleys that evoke the ancient traditions of the past.

Let's remember. The craft stores of the past, are testimony of history, culture and tradition of a city, the vitality of a place, the spirit of a city, are living monuments of the past, a unique cultural heritage, are points of reference.

Very often families of artisans and merchants have handed down the profession, ensuring customers a high level of research and quality. Only a few decades ago to indicate a place to be, often not a street or a square was mentioned, but the name of some store that everyone knew by collective memory (Chifari, 2019).

I shudder to think of seeing cold outlets or soulless places to consume junk food spring up and take the place of the charming stores of yesteryear. Have you ever contemplated those fabulous sixteenth century palaces or those extraordinary nineteenth century structures with early twentieth century furnishings?

Have you ever stopped to observe those centuries-old historic stores that retain the charm of past centuries, with their period furnishings, antique signs, fixtures, frescoes and paintings on the vaults?

Before I start talking about mastermind groups, collaborative networks, virtual teams and remote work, I bow. I bow before all the families who have given their lives for generations to their business, passing down quality, art and culture.

Thanks to their activities, they allow city centers to preserve their historical memory and with their "romantic air of other times", they give value to the community and the urban fabric. These activities must be protected and defended.

Man must be able to find a balance, the right harmony, the right alchemy, between the culture of the past and the innovation and progress of the future. We need to be able to take advantage of the opportunities offered by the online world, but at the same time not forget how beautiful real life is compared to the virtual world. Thanks to the opportunities that the online world offers, it is possible to have more free time and higher economic income, which allows us to better enjoy the beauty of the offline world.

Everyone can take advantage of the opportunities offered by the online world, including historic shops, which can make their business known worldwide, establish collaborations and international partnerships, and even "monetize" their knowledge by creating video courses and books to pass on their culture and tradition.

I hope that humanity will become capable of finding the right balance between the two realities, with the hope of seeing all the historic shops that still carry out their activities flourish.

Give Your Business a Boost

As mentioned, the positives of remote work cannot be underestimated and not only does it improve the lives of employers but of employees too. Employees are found to be more productive when working from their location of choice due to a lack of stress that may manifest in workplaces or on the commute to and from. The stress often found in workplaces results in a slower output of ideas that often lack an edge of creativity as well. When this stress is eliminated it allows for better focus, collaboration, and overall better outcomes of projects. An improved mental capacity of employees will lead to improved communication among members. The concept of peer-to-peer guidance and collaboration may be the edge your business needs. Keep reading to find out just how you can get your teams to work 'smart!'.

There are instances where remote work can worsen productivity and business communication. Others where it can put your mental and physical health at risk and damage your brain. We'll go over all of this as well so that you can increase productivity and work remotely in a healthy and profitable way.

1. Smart Working

The goals of your business may become convoluted due to the ever-changing working culture. Therefore, to get back that edge, the first thing that can be implemented is smart working. The transformation of technology that has ushered in the peak of the digital age is an unstoppable force. Smart work can be defined as a model of remote working using its opportunities to create a flexible, collaborative, and efficient work environment.

The purpose of smart working is to be able to equip employees with the skills and tools that will allow them to be effective and efficient. Skills and tools vary and can include but are not limited to, the work culture, leadership styles that employees interact with, and the type of technology and access to resources that they can use.

The more control and autonomy an employee can exert on the factors that allow them to do their job creates an environment wherein they can optimize their efforts toward projects.

So smart working is a flexible approach that relies on the trust and accountability of workers who must comply with company guidelines. Employees can do the work in different locations and are usually evaluated and managed based on their results.

Technology plays an essential role in smart working as it provides flexibility, which allows growth and innovation in businesses. Using smart work, a model of remote work that integrates new technologies with existing ones, work that is meaningful and fulfilling is achieved. The idea behind smart working is to automate the work as much as possible to maintain consistency. The set of practices that often characterize smart working are the flexible hours, location, and ability to share responsibility in real-time. This allows projects to be completed more efficiently as well as maintain a consistency that is sometimes lost when teams are not working together physically. Given the recent changes we are experiencing, remote working has become necessary and has resulted in employees searching for meaningful work that can be done from anywhere, this makes using the business model of smart working an essential tool.

This chapter will address the benefits of smart working as well as any disadvantages that may be experienced by this model of working. Additionally, tips on how to make smart working work for your business will be shared.

Fig. 1: Tools used in smart working.

Benefits of Smart Working

Increases Productivity

Employees have the flexibility to decide when, where, and how they want to work, leading to the best possible work they can produce. Additionally, due to meetings being online they are generally shorter and more efficient, saving the time of both managers and employees and giving them more time to carry out other work tasks. Using technology also means no unnecessary breaks, which often form part of office culture. You can stay more focused because you are preserved from distractions in the workplace, such as disturbing voices and noises from colleagues.

Management Improvement

Now that employees are able to manage their own time and potentially produce their best possible work, managers do not spend time hovering hour after hour. This creates time for managers to focus on the objective of projects rather than merely on those doing the work. They are now able to more clearly direct their projects toward the most important objectives of the company.

The Environment

Smart work not only impacts businesses and people but also the environment at large. Transport, both individual and public, causes pollution. With companies using smart work and many working from home, transportation is cut down and thus pollution levels are too. Reducing unnecessary car trips positively impacts the environment, and avoiding the stress of traffic is good for health.

Disadvantages of Smart Working

Finances

While smart working can reduce costs for the company, it can sometimes put a strain on employees' finances, depending on their home office situations. Companies will be saving on the costs of the upkeep of physical spaces. However, employees will have initial costs for their new, home workspaces. They may also incur additional costs for electricity or raised internet bills due to faster speeds required for work.

Decreased Productivity

If there is no plan or schedule for how work is to be divided or deadlines for goals to be met, smart work does have the potential to be unproductive. This could result in a quantity over the quality situation with employees being paid but project outcomes not materializing.

It will also serve to develop the ability to stay focused and resist the distractions that technological devices offer. Attention is power. People spend 46.9% of their waking hours thinking about something other than what they're doing, and this mind-wandering typically makes them unhappy (Bradt, 2010). The digital world only amplifies this phenomenon of "inattention to the here and now", putting us in contact with other worlds and other people, more or less distant (Carciofi, 2017). Companies will need to invest in training to help their teams manage digital distractions.

Isolation

Smart work is done from remote locations and as such coworkers do not interact with each other the way they usually would. This could lead to feelings of isolation from their colleagues and cause a loss of identification with the company. This loss of identification could also isolate employees from their work and distract them from the objectives of the project. This could also result in a decrease in productivity and potentially subpar work.

Hyperconnection, Workaholism and Burnout Syndrome

Many Smart Workers develop a hyperconnection, they feel an excessive need to stay constantly connected to the internet to do their job. They feel compelled to be available at all times of the day and over time become unable to disconnect from the internet.

In most cases, they don't notice the time ticking away, become detached from the real world and end up working more than they should. This overwork often causes psychophysical stress. There is now evidence that mobile devices can increase stress levels.

In more extreme cases, one can develop work addictions such as workaholism (a combination of the words work and alcoholism), "the compulsion or the uncontrollable need to work incessantly" (Oates, 1971), an addiction to one's work activity. [1]

[1]. What are the differences between work engagement, work addiction, and workaholism? Both terms can be depicted, respectively, as the pathological and the healthy form of heavy work investment.

Workaholism and work engagement are not clearly and adequately distinguished by scholars and researchers as they appear to show some overlapping features (Di Stefano & Gaudiino, 2019).

These terms are not yet clearly and adequately distinguished by scholars and researchers as they seem to exhibit some overlapping features. They are forms of overwork, and are often used interchangeably in the literature. Although workaholism and work addiction overlap at some points, some components of their meaning may differ (Griffiths et al., 2018).

It was proposed by some authors that work addiction was a

psychological construct, whereas workaholism was a more generic term indicating everyday work-related behavior rather than pathology (Clark et al., 2020; Griffiths et al., 2018).It is possible to disentangle the differences between workaholism and work addiction by paying attention not only to their composition but also to the factors determining them (Morkevičiūtė & Endriulaitiene, 2021).

In theory, working more should lead to higher productivity, but research in psychology and medicine shows otherwise (Carciofi, 2017). There is a positive correlation between increased work hours and increased problems related to headache, insomnia, and burnout syndrome.

Burnout is a psychological syndrome of job stress, a state of depersonalization, personal derealization and exhaustion on an emotional, physical and mental level. Job stress naturally lowers the immune system and increases the risk of heart disease, high blood pressure, obesity, diabetes and cancer.

Being online all the time is harmful. Many people begin to exhibit obsessive and pathological behaviors, such as checking email inboxes all day or constantly picking up their smartphones to check notifications and what's happening on social networks. Those who work on tech devices in the evening are also at risk of altering their circadian sleep patterns.

I'd like to point out, though, that the problem isn't smart working, it's how you work in smart working. So, I still reiterate the importance of corporate training. Companies will need to invest in training to teach their teams how to work in smart working.

Fig. 2: Disadvantages of smart work can include decreased motivation and productivity.

Smart Working Tips

Smart working is based in the virtual world and this can be difficult to get used to. However, treating flexibility and virtuality as the default for all employees will ensure this to be the basis of the company's culture. The result of this will be efficient and effective smart working. Additionally, when assigning tasks, the flexibility offered to employees should be taken into consideration. This means creating projects that can be done using the expertise of the whole team and ensuring that all employees are using the smart work model.

The smart working model has its foundation in trust, and management should exhibit this by allowing employees to work without constant hovering or bombardment of online meetings. Rather, checking in when necessary and having realistic deadlines will promote a culture of trust and result in the best project outcomes. This tool allows managers to judge the quality of an employee based on the work they put out rather than their presence or having them "show up."

To ensure that the smart work model is being used to its full potential, managers should keep an eye out for any problems that may arise. Managers will have to use their people skills. Solutions should be found through honest and open communication between employees and management. This will allow smart working to continue and build the basis of trust that is needed for employees to have flexibility.

Sometimes it will also be very important to create situations to bring the whole team together live. The combination of office and digital experience gives the company a greater possibilities of being effective.

Even at a distance, it is a good practice to have "digital coffees" to keep in touch with people. This is essential, it is a way to carry on the "old office conversations".

Trusting people is key, as is making sure to give employees all the tools they need to do their jobs at their best.

So, from a technological point of view, it is necessary to do a good company checkup:

- *Are you confident that everyone involved in the company has the same experience from home as they do in the office, in terms of applications, software, processes, invoicing, customer engagement and communication?*

- *Are the company's processes and systems secure?*

- *How can this experience be guaranteed to accelerate innovation in all the things you do?*

The company should take care of providing all the necessary information and tools to help take advantage of this way of working and several times I have talked about offering specific training courses.

Furthermore, smart workers will have to:

- *Develop the competence to work in smart working. Some people are ready to do it, others are less cable. It takes time to learn.*

- *Create an environment where one feel good. Feeling good in your own home is very important. If you are in an environment where you feel good, you can face all work problems with a better attitude.*

- *Get used to being judged by results. Many people are used to understanding work as a series of efforts and activities that one does, regardless of the results. It is necessary to pay less attention to the activities performed and to focus more on the results achieved.*

- *Understand that by working in smart working you are no longer "competing" with professionals from one's own city, but with people from all over the world. You become easily replaceable. This is why you have to be good at what you do, you have to be so good as to be "irreplaceable".*

- *Develop self-discipline, a sense of responsibility and become good at motivating yourself.*

- *Develop great organizational skills to find the right balance between work and private life. So become good at drawing a line between private and working life. It can help to set precise timetables, keep a schedule and have a calendar.*

- *Know how to take breaks without overdoing it.*

The management will need to take into account that:

- *Firing becomes easier and less traumatic because lacking a live relationship, less deep relationships develop.*

- *It's important to understand when it's time to keep team morale up and motivated.*

- *If you have people on your team scattered around the world, it is important to consider the time zone when scheduling meetings and work deadlines.*

If management notices that smart working lowers productivity throughout the team, then there is a problem upstream in staff selection. If you have hired people who only work for a paycheck at the end of the month, you will have to do things differently. Most people just work to bring home a paycheck; they don't do the work they love to do. They do that job because they have no other alternative.

Companies need to understand that it is important to hire people based on their values: people's values must be aligned with company values. But we're going to touch on other issues here, which are beyond the scope of this book.

For more information on other fundamental business topics to achieve maximum profits you can take advantage of the training courses of Zeloni Corporation, my training company dedicated to Business Applied Mental Sciences. You'll also find many other courses on our Business Galaxy platform.

zeloni.eu

businessgalaxy.training

Another important tip I feel like giving you is about isolation. The time you gain from working online from home can be spent meeting live friends and playing with them. The problem of isolation in smart working is often a false problem resulting from an approximate, incomplete and superficial vision of reality; because if working in smart working makes you be more "isolated from your colleagues" but more "close to your real friends", the problem of isolation does not exist. This depends on how you spend the time you have saved.

We also need to remember that we have a right to disconnect from the Internet. Being online all the time is wrong. Life is not just work! Disconnecting from technology is fundamental, it's important not to lose touch with reality.

So we have to be good at balancing online work with real life, we have to carve out spaces for reflection, meditation, thinking, and contemplating what's around us. These are all fundamental processes for staying connected to ourselves and maintaining self-awarness. So, get out of artificial environments to be in touch with nature, breathe in the open air, devote time to physical activity and find time to eat calmly and quietly, without haste. Body, Mind and Spirit will benefit greatly.

2. Remote Working

Now that we understand what smart working is and how to integrate it with current business models, it is time to discuss remote work. It has gained popularity recently and studies have shown that the preference for working remotely is only rising (PMI.it, 2021). However, before we go any further, it's best that we understand what exactly remote working is.

If you want to operate under an online business model, that means you must have a system where everyone is working remotely. Remote working, also known as telecommuting or working from home (WFH), is the practice of employees working from a location of their choosing rather than commuting to a centralized one like an office building. While WFH may be the most common name for remote working, from here on out this book will only be using the term remote working. The reason for that is that remote working can occur anywhere, it is not limited to the home, and therefore remote working is the most accurate name. And you must also be careful not to confuse it with telecommuting, which often has the same time rigidity as corporate offices.

Remote working relies entirely on employees working away from the office, and unlike smart working, does not rely on particular company culture. It has become an attractive opportunity for freelancers, temps, and agencies as it relies on the quality of your work and offers the most flexibility in terms of hours. To get everyone up to speed on the topic, the advantages and disadvantages of this model will be covered, as well as a few tips for how to improve performance.

Benefits of Remote Working

Flexibility and Freedom

The most apparent benefit of remote working is that employees have the freedom and flexibility to set their own hours. When employees can work around their own schedules, they decide when work gets done thereby allowing them to set schedules that maximize productivity.

This can alleviate some of the pressure that comes with having a set schedule and revolves around commuting, office culture, and the constant presence of a manager when trying to make deadlines.

Mental Health Improvement

There are always instances of stress whether you enjoy your job or not. The impact that work may have on your employees' mental health could be detrimental to your company. Commuting to work has the largest effect on one's mental health (Reynolds, n.d.). With remote working, your employees will not have to commute thereby removing this stress from their lives. Their overall mental health will improve with the lack of stress increasing their potential productivity when they are allowed to work from the location of their choosing.

Working from home also reduces other work-related stressors that include but are not limited to, office politics or even colleagues who may interrupt workflow. Remote working removes these distractions and allows an employee to create their own safe and comfortable workspace that they are able to thrive in.

Reduced Costs

Remote working reduces costs for both employees and

employers. Employees can save on commute costs every day now that they are working from home. Additionally, they are able to save on childcare costs due to the flexibility of their schedule that allows them to prioritize differently. This does not impact the company as when employees are allowed to choose the variables that affect their work they will structure them to maximize productivity in smaller amounts of time. Employers benefit too as they do not have to pay for an expensive building as well as any additional costs such as water and electricity bills.

Work From Anywhere

Another benefit of the remote working is that people can work from anywhere. When the company isn't bound by a physical location they can hire people from anywhere in the world. This has the potential to drastically increase the size of the qualified job pool. It also has the potential to impact communities that are struggling or have traditionally been classified as lower class.

With the ability to choose your location those in rural or underdeveloped areas are able to engage in work that leaves them feeling fulfilled while impacting those that are not near them. This will allow communities to experience both economic and social change thereby uplifting not only a company's impact but so too that of the community.

Fig. 3: Remote working allows employees to pick their location.

Increase in Productivity

Remote working allows for flexible hours allowing employees to work whenever they choose. This will boost productivity as employees will work when they are best able to perform. Also, employees will generally want to work the shortest possible amount while still producing results. This allows work to be completed around the clock from various locations, meaning that a company's goals are constantly being met.

Not having to reach office daily offers benefits both in terms of time saved and stress reduction. Both of these factors contribute to increased productivity.

Disadvantages of Remote Working

Employee Disconnect

However, there are some disadvantages to the remote working model too that should be noted. Working from home can also lead to a feeling of isolation in employees and a disconnect between employee and employer. When people don't see each other every day, it can be difficult to feel like you're all a part of the same team. Additionally, the lack of presence can impact employees if they don't feel they have enough interaction with their managers it may stunt their career growth. This can lead to feelings of hesitation to join a company that has a remote working model.

Unbalanced Work/Life

The balance between work and personal life can be tricky even when not working remotely. When working remotely there is a possibility that the lines between the two may become blurred and an imbalance may occur. When your home is the location that you do work it is easy to begin overworking as you simply wish to have tasks completed, regardless of whether you are on the clock. The lack of physical boundary between where one works and where they spend their leisure time could indicate that there is no boundary and cause employees to feel disconnected from their leisure.

Distractions

While remote work allows for employees to create their best possible work location oftentimes this means an employee's home. As this is a personal space there are many crossovers between personal life and work-life and this can be overwhelming to employees and distract them from the task at hand.

Disrupted Work Culture

With employees working remotely there is a decrease in physical interactions between coworkers. This can impact the relationships that form amongst employees and team members or rather the lack thereof. Despite there being tools and technology that enable work to be effective it doesn't foster relationships and this could impact work culture. Without the bonds that form between coworkers and managers with their employees work productivity may be stunted.

Remote Working Tips

While the disadvantages to remote working may seem dreary here are a few tips to make the remote working model work for your company. Encourage employees to establish a comfortable space and a set-out area specifically for working in. The creation of a designated workspace, although at home, will solidify a boundary for working as well as an area that is free of distractions; it will allow employees to work productively as well as maintain a work/life balance.

Create a consistent and plan out a schedule for remote working. That means setting out tasks and scheduling realistic deadlines so that employees are able to produce work without feeling overwhelmed. It is necessary to plan a schedule that is built around the work being remote so that online meetings can still conduct a sense of authority and allow employees to feel secure in their work.

Fig. 4: Communication is key in a successful remote working model.

In addition to a schedule, communication is key. An essential aspect of remote working is the ability of coworkers and managers and employees to communicate with each other. In some cases, overcommunication is advised as it is better for everyone to know too much than not enough. This too will help alleviate the sense of isolation or a lack of relationships that may be characteristic of remote working. Communication will also help with achieving goals and staying on task to meet the company's objectives.

Lastly, it is important to encourage employees to take breaks. It is easy to overwork when working remotely as you'll want to keep completing tasks. However, to maintain consistent productivity, breaks are necessary. This will also help to maintain a good work/life balance and leave everyone feeling overall better thereby allowing the remote working model to be successful.

How to Take Effective Breaks (and Be More Productive)

When work intensifies we tend to work harder than we should, pushing our bodies and minds to the limit. The problem is that without any restorative break to recharge our energy, we are less efficient, more mistakes are made and we lower our productivity.

Our body must be listened to, it often sends us signals that we need a break. We must learn to respect the natural rhythms of our organism, which naturally goes into "pause" many times a day to regulate our psychophysical system.

In these moments of pause, we need to put the outside world on hold. It is no accident that the original meaning of "wait" is "turn the soul to" Every pause becomes an opportunity to take care of ourselves. We must shift the beacon of attention from the outer world to the inner world.

Without these rejuvenating moments, there can be no extreme productivity. The mistake that many people make is sacrificing rest in the name of productivity. But working hard doesn't always equate to producing great results. Rest is one of the keys to being super productive. When rest is lacking or of poor quality, productivity and creativity drop dramatically.

Instead of scheduling your rest around your work, you should learn to manage your work around your rest, and the good news is that smart and remote working allow you to do this. Learn to get organized, plan your rest and relaxation time in advance, and add work commitments around your sacred moments. You'll experience the day with more joy, which will allow you to recharge your physical, mental, and emotional batteries.

But in addition to rest and relaxation, small work breaks are also important. Research on alternating work-rest for better performance converges on the fact that the body needs a break every 90-120 minutes (Carciofi. 2017).

The break must represent a true interruption of what you are doing. There has to be a drastic change that fosters the experience of interruption. You have to stop what you were doing and focus on something completely different, so you have to do the opposite of what you were doing at work:

- *If you've been sitting the whole time, take a walk, get some exercise or stretch.*
- *If you had to speak in a meeting, spend moments in silence.*
- *if you've been working in silence the whole time, start talking or put on some music.*
- *if you have been working online, the break must be offline.*
- *If you've been working indoors, go outside, get some sunshine and fresh air.*

Here's what you don't have to do on your break:

- *If you were typing on the computer, don't start reading*

something. Beware of information overload!

- *If you've been working on the computer, don't check your email or social media.*

- *Don't eat junk food, or foods with excess sugar that later lead to a drop in energy.*

- *Don't stick to your smartphone like a dopamine-seeking junkie.*

Do you remember that you need to shift the spotlight of attention from the outer world to the inner world? Enjoy the break without the technology! Every time you decide to give yourself a quality break, you are taking care of yourself.

How to Increase Productivity

First thing in the morning, work on your most important task. Immerse yourself in the task and eliminate distractions. Enjoy the process. Don't do anything else until this is done. Give yourself a short break and then start on your next most important task.

It is helpful to create focus time blocks to increase productivity. A focus block is a dedicated chunk of time that you set aside to work on a task. When you are working on a task in a time block, you turn off all other distractions.

Depending on the type of work you're doing and the concentration required, you can create focused blocks of 90, 50 or 25 minutes. For example:

- 90 minutes + 20 minute break
- 50 minutes + 10 minute break
- 25 minutes + 5 minute break

Blocks of 50 are recommended because after 40-45 minutes there is a physiological decline in both information retention, energy, and therefore productivity (Formisano, 2016). But sometimes we can be more performant with 90, sometimes with 25. This also depends on whether it is morning or afternoon. The important thing is to take a break just before the physiological decline arrives.

So, get used from today to plan your work, set priorities and then devote yourself to the most important task. Focus solely on it and don't do anything else until you have finished it.

This means working in "single-handing" mode. Select a task, start working on it, and force yourself to complete it before moving on to the next task.

Single-Handing

This principle was popularized by time management expert Alan Lakein, his studies revealed that every time you put aside a job and devote yourself to something else, you lose momentum and rhythm, but not only that: you also lose track of where you were in doing that job (Tracy, 2013).

When you take it back, you will have to revisit the work you have done to get back on track, and this process can take up to 500% of the time it would take to complete a task if you did it from start to finish. Also Brian Tracy supports the single-handing principle that can reduce the time it takes to complete important task as much as 80% and significantly improve the quality of the finished work (Tracy, 2013).

Increase Concentration

If we are able to increase our concentration, we can increase our productivity. Staying focused is very important. As Earl

Nightingale told us that, every great accomplishment in life has been preceded by a long, sustained period of concentration.

Daniel Goleman said that our attention is not like a balloon that can expand to encompass more things at a time, but can rather be compared to a thin tube, which can only lead a liquid in one direction: instead of dividing it between two activities, we oscillate rapidly between the two, a passage which in any case inolves a weakening compared to full concentration.

When we get to work on our most important task, we must be able to persevere without letting anything or anyone distract us.

> "Focus is a matter of deciding what things you're not going to do"
>
> John Carmack

If there's one thing to avoid, it is multitasking, which is nothing more than "task-shifting," the constant switching from one job to another. This is an unnecessary waste of energy. Many people think that multitasking is something efficient, but multitasking is neither efficient nor effective; Leo Babauta points out that it is less efficient, due to need to switch gears for each new task and then switch back again. Multitasking is more complicated, and thus leaves you more prone to errors and stress (Babauta, 2009). It has also been found that higher stressed people in multitasking environments use more anger in their emails (Akbar et al., 2019).

Studies now have shown that humans actually can do two things or more at once, for example walking and talking, eating something and reading; but we cannot focus on two things at once (Keller, 2018).

"To do two things at once is to do neither."

Publilio Sirio

If you try to do two things at once, you won't do any of them well. As Steve Uzzell said, multitasking is merely the opportunity to screw up more than one thing at a time.

The fact is, our brains are not designed to work this way. Research conducted at Stanford University shows that people who multitask are actually less productive than those who don't and are significantly worse at switching off from a certain task and switching to another one (Bradberry, n.d.). Their quality of work is, as a result, far less than those who refuse to multitask. What's worse is that multitasking actually reduces your productivity over time (Zeloni Magelli, 2020).

Biologically, this makes sense since you're weakening your brain steadily over time and can hardly expect it to be able to keep up (Zeloni Magelli, 2020). Cognitive impairment from multitasking is not temporary. Researchers at the University of Sussex in the UK compared the amount of time people spend on multiple devices (such as texting while watching TV) to MRI scans of their brains. They found that high multitaskers had less brain density in the anterior cingulate cortex, a region responsible for empathy as well as cognitive and emotional control (Bradberry, n.d.).

The lead author of this study - Neuroscientist Kep Kee Loh - warns us: "I feel that it is important to create an awareness that the way we are interacting with the devices might be changing the way we think and these changes might be occurring at the level of brain structure."

We live in a multitasking world. As Gary Keller argues, it's not that we have too little time to do all the things that need to be done, it's that we feel we need to do too many things in the time we have. The net result is a low quality of work that only increases the number of things you need to get done, the exact opposite of what was the primary objective.

All of this causes stress, and the immune system weakens.

Stress also lowers our energy levels, when we have low energy our concentration disappears, and productivity plummets.

Focus is your most important tool in becoming more effective. Try to stay focused on the task at hand. Focus on now. Focusing on the present can do a lot for you. It helps to reduce stress. It helps you enjoy life to the fullest, and increase your effectiveness (Babauta, 2009).

"With the past, I have nothing to do; nor with the future. I live now"

Ralph Waldo Emerson

Email Management

Much productive time is wasted on email management, so it's important to address this topic. Workplace environments are characterized by frequent interruptions that can lead to stress. However, measures of stress due to interruptions are typically obtained through self-reports, which can be affected by memory and emotional biases (Akbar et al., 2019).

A major source of interruptions in the workplace is email.

Studies have found the longer daily time spent on email, the lower was perceived productivity and the higher the measured stress. (Mark et al., 2016), and that increased productivity and decreased stress can be achieved by limiting the amount one accesses email, managing inbox size, and utilizing good email etiquette (Armstrong, 2017).

In addition, it was found that while intensive email use may harm ability to concentrate, may increase forgetfulness and inability to solve problems at work effectively (Franssila et al., 2014). and that email overload can generate so-called "technostress", that is the inability to cope with information and communication technology which may result in stress and burnout (Lowrie, 2019).[2]

[2]. Technostress is based on the root concept of stress (Brod, 1984), including: (1) the internal state of the organism (or strain); (2) an external event (or stressor); and (3) an experience that arises from an ongoing transaction between a person and the environment. This is further derived from general stress in the workplace, which is considered as the harmful physical and emotional responses that occur when job requirements do not match the worker's capabilities, resources, and needs (Bondanini et al. 2020).

It has been defined as any negative impact on attitudes, thoughts, behaviours, or body physiology that is caused either directly or indirectly by technology (Weil & Rosen, 1997) and even as the stress that users experience as a result of application multitasking, constant connectivity, information overload, frequent system upgrades and consequent uncertainty, continual relearning and consequent job-related insecurities, and technical problems associated with the organizational use of ICT (Tarafdar et al. 2010).

Technostress affects job satisfaction, organizational commitment, and employee outcomes; it is also considered to be a negative psychological state related to current or future use (or abuse) of technology (Salanova et al. 2014) that has a large social impact in our lives. In fact, scholars point out that the technology could be a threat to our established set of norms and patterns of behaviour which make us adaptive in our environment, and therefore brings negative emotional reactions, anxiety and fear. This ambivalence is expressed by technophobia (rejection and/or avoidance of technology) and technophilia (attraction and enthusiastic adoption of technology). (Bondanini et al. 2020; Martínez-Córcoles, 2017).

Despite its benefits for both organizations and workers, remote working entails negative consequences, such as technostress (Molino et al. 2020) .

A group of researchers (Molino et al. 2020) points out that requests to workers and workload levels need to be monitored by supervisors and managers. The "always on" working practice, encouraged by remote working, challenges employees in terms of mental and physical fatigue. Because of the features of remote working, which is mainly a home-based activity, organizational demands tend to exceed normal working hours and normal workload with undebatable consequences for individual and organizational performance and wellbeing (Molino et al. 2020).

About a good **email etiquette**, Alessio Carciofi — an expert in digital transformation — gives us some tips:

- *Only access our email inboxes at certain times or blocks of the day. And a few times a day. With this "block" (batching) approach, we are able to save time and increase our focus.*

- *Establish a time limit for each block/time we access email. This way we will only handle the most important emails and not have time for junk emails.*

- *Don't keep the email window open when we are doing other tasks.*

- *Unsubscribe from newsletters that do not interest us and delete all push notifications.*

People who primarily check email in response to email notifications report lower productivity than those who self-interrupt to check email (Mark et al., 2016), this is also why batching is useful.[3]

3. Batching refers to a mode of "bundled execution", "task aggregation", "lotting" or "block division". It is a technique used to increase productivity that consists of grouping tasks of the same type to be performed in a given block of time. This technique is also applied to email management.

With this approach you will only think about your inbox at certain times. If you check your email constantly, even quickly, your attention will be diverted from the task at hand. Even if you go right back to your task, your inbox continues to take up space in your mind. This approach helps you limit distractions, maintain focus, and waste less time. You'll increase your efficiency.

A study commissioned by Hewlett-Packard found that workers who were continually distracted by calls, emails and phones lowered their IQ by an average of 10 points (Carciofi, 2017).

Cal Newport, after studying the phenomenon of network switching with psychologists and neuroscientists, confirms that "Our minds cannot do these rapid context shifts from one thing to an inbox back to the one thing, back to an inbox,". Network switching can take the brain between 5 to 15 minutes, This constant switching exhausts our brains and also causes anxiety (Newport, 2021).[4]

[4]. In computer science, network switching is the process of channeling data received from any number of input ports to another designated port that will transmit the data to its desired destination. The device through with the input data passes is called a switch (Griffin, 2019).

After a distraction, it takes about 15 minutes to resume interrupted work, and 24 to return to focus mode. This is no way to work. We've already talked about the negative effects of multitasking. People are not good at quickly switching back and forth between tasks; the human brain cannot perform this process quickly. Constantly switching from one task to another is not healthy.

"Email is not a technical problem, it's a people problem"

Merlin Mann

E-mail is a very widely used tool in business life because it is very effective. It has solved many problems related to the old tools to send messages, such as telegraph, telex, AUTODIN, fax and answering machine.

The problem is its use. We have already ascertained that technology affects human behavior. The constant and compulsive checking of email is sabotaging the minds of workers: mental fatigue, clouded mind, loss of mental clarity, stress, distractions and loss of concentration.

It can help to have a **method for processing emails quickly**. Leo Babauta — writer and author of the Zen Habits blog — gives us some tips in this one:

- *Work your way from top o bottom, one e-mail at a time.*

- *Open each e-mail and dispose of it immediately. Your choices: delete, archive (for later reference), reply quickly*

> *(and archive or delete the message), put on your to-do list (and archive or delete the message), do the task immediately (If it requires two minutes or less — then archive or delete), or forward (and archive or delete).*

With this method, the email is ultimately archived or deleted. And he recommends removing it from the inbox immediately and never leaving it there. This is something to do quickly and then move on to the next email. Don't be afraid to delete an email, what's the worst that will happen if I delete this? If the answer isn't bad, just delete it and move on. With good practice, you can plow through a couple dozen message very quickly (Babauta, 2009).

It will help you save time, energy, physical and mental resources to even **not respond to emails.** Not responding to an email may seem rude, but sometimes it is necessary. We can't devote our time to everyone. Time is a very precious and limited resource. Honoring the extraordinary gift of life also means making the best use of our time. Therefore, it is a divine duty not to waste time responding to emails that do not bring value to our lives.

What is the worst thing that can happen if you don't respond? Is it something you might be interested in? Is it an incomplete and approximate email? Is it ambiguous and confusing? Some emails are not worthy of a response. If an email is taking valuable mental resources away from you, don't respond. Value your time!

Finally: no emails on nights and weekends!

Learn to Manage Distractions

If you work in a noisy environment, you should try to double your concentration by ignoring the surrounding noises. Being able to concentrate in the midst of the indoors is an indication of selective attention, the neural ability to focus on a single thing while ignoring a sea of other stimuli, any of which might catch your attention (Goleman, 2014).

Primarily, there are sensory distractions and emotional distractions.

Sensory distractions are easier to cope with: for example, while you're reading this book, you're ignoring the clothes on your skin. or the pages of paper you're touching, these are just a small part of the countless stimuli that your brain removes from the continuous stream of background sensations involving the five senses.

Emotional distractions, on the other hand, are more dangerous. It doesn't matter what you're doing, but if you hear your name mentioned — which has an emotional appeal to you — your attention will abandon what it's doing and head to the voice of the person who said your name.

Even people with good concentration skills can succumb to emotional distractions. For example, if you've had a fight with a loved one, it will be difficult to keep your mind clear.

The problem is that when we lose concentration, our performance suffers a drastic drop and we are less productive. Research from Harvard Business School identified reduced creative activity when work is continually interrupted by any type of distraction (Carciofi, 2017).

Enhancing our concentration is critical. Because to focus we must also silence our emotional distractions, the neural circuitry of selective attention includes that for inhibition of emotions: this means that people who concentrate better are relatively immune to emotional turmoil, have less difficulty keeping themselves imperturbable in moments of crisis, and remain stable in the midst of life's emotional flux (Goleman, 2014).

Goleman tells us that the effort to focus on one thing while ignoring everything else represents a kind of conflict for the brain. In these mental conflicts, the role of mediator is exerted by the anterior cingulate cortex (ACC), which identifies these problems and instructs other parts of the brain to solve them. To maintain focus on an object, the ACC appeals to the prefrontal areas responsible for cognitive control, which silence distracting elements and amplify those to which we want to devote all our attention.

To facilitate these mental and brain processes, it will be very helpful for you to have an empowering environment around you.

The Empowering Environment

Your environment must support your goals. Your environment consists of everything you experience every day: places, social aspects, things, tools and people around you. You must pay attention. Anyone and anything at any time can steal your attention and take away your power.

First, have a clean and tidy desk. It allows you to have a clear mind and focus only on the task at hand. It gives you a greater sense of calm and serenity to work in a neat and tidy place without distractions and objects taking up space in your mind. Less mental clutter, more resources for our cognitive processes.

First, make sure you are working in a **clean and tidy work environment.** Clutter is full of potential distractions. It takes your attention away from your most important task and directs it to other worlds, such as memories, unfinished tasks or other things to do. A tidy environment will improve your energy and mood, drive your motivation and you will be more satisfied.

It will help you create a **minimalist desk**. It will allow you to have a clearer mind, so you can focus better on the task in front of you. A clear desk helps concentration, you will be able to work more lucidly.

Remember that every day is an amazing day for new ideas and opportunities. A cluttered desk with work from previous days anchors you to the past. Instead with a "new" desk every day, you'll be encouraged to new possibilities; even if you're working on a project from previous days, you'll see things in a new light and it will help you innovate.

Here are a few tips to get you started:

- *Reduce the items in your workspace. Remove anything that is not essential. There will not be unnecessary items taking up space in your mind.*

- *Sort the materials in your drawers. You don't have to have things or projects on your desk. You'll have things or projects handy in your drawers, but only the most important task on your desk.*

- *Don't leave projects unfinished. They consume mental resources in the background. If they require little time to complete, complete them! If not, put them in the drawer.*

- *Declutter your desktop. It will help you limit distractions and won't cloud your mental clarity.*

- *Before you end your workday, get everything in order.*

All of this will give you a greater sense of calm and serenity and you will have a more efficient mind. Less mental clutter means more resources for our cognitive processes.

Another tip is to use a **dedicated computer** just for work. Don't work with your personal devices. I also recommend that you have a dedicated device (desktop computer, laptop, or tablet) for each type of task. For example: 1 just for graphics and video, 1 for writing, 1 for email management, 1 for social networking, and so on.

This will help you limit distractions and focus better on the task at hand. If you want to go further, I recommend having **dedicated rooms** for each type of task and assignment as well. This will give you the amazing power to get into the flow of extreme productivity right away.

What's most important is that you are picking a spot that you can devote specifically to that activity. If you do that work in the same spot where you play, that's where your mind will go. Pick a place that gives you complete mental clarity so that you don't have anything to focus on other than that task. Somehow the places are real anchors that activate certain mental and emotional states (Zeloni Magelli, 2020).

Places are energy fields. The energies of your thoughts stay in your room. Think of the benefit of accessing that place and being able to quickly tune into those frequencies required to perform that task. This strategy also allows you to facilitate context shifts and network switching. You'll be much more productive and experience legendary mental clarity when performing tasks.

Your rooms need to have quality air. The air we breathe is very important for our health. Our psychophysical well-being also depends on the air we breathe. That's why I recommend that you have **air-purifying plants** in your work environment.

Unfortunately, there are chemicals in indoor environments that come from foundations, walls, furniture, plastics, adhesives, paints, electronics and cleaning products such as: benzene, trichloroethylene, formaldehyde, pentachlorophenol, chloromethane, ammonium chloride, carbon monoxide, acetone, radon, xylene, toluene, and others; are volatile organic compounds.[5]

5. Volatile organic compounds (VOC's) are an extensive class of chemical compounds which exist as gasses at ambient standard temperature and pressure. Are compounds like acetone, benzene and formaldehyde that are emitted as gases and can cause short- and long-term health effects when inhaled (American Chemical Society, 2016).

The health risks associated with this broad class of chemicals range from tiredness and acute nausea to central nervous system damage and cancer (Jones, 2015).

Dr. Vadoud Niri of the State University of New York at Oswego confirm that inhaling large amounts of VOCs can lead some people to develop sick building syndrome, which reduces productivity and can even cause dizziness, asthma or allergies (American Chemical Society, 2016).

The most effective solution is offered by Mother Nature: plants. Using plants to remove chemicals from indoor air is called biofiltration or phytoremediation. Phytoremediation is the process by which plants and their root microbes remove contaminants from both air and water. Plant biofiltration is a promising technology that can help solve widespread global problems caused by air pollution (Wolverton & Nelson 2020).

VOC's are found in much higher concentrations in indoor environments than outdoors, with particularly high concentrations in new buildings. Certain plants have the capacity to remove airborne VOC's, but the efficacy of removal depends on chemical compounds and the mechanism of uptake utilized by each plant. (Jones, 2015). Plant roots and their associated microorganisms then destroy the pathogenic viruses, bacteria, and the organic chemicals, eventually converting all of these air pollutants into new plant tissue (Wolverton et al., 1989).

Fortunately, there are some species of plants that are able to combat indoor air pollution. The plants you'll find on this list are capable of filtering out numerous types of VOCs. VOC reduction varied, but ubiquitous among all plants, some of them — such us cactus — even excel at absorbing electrosmog:

- *Bromeliad - Guzmania lingulata*

- *Areca palm - Dypsis lutescens*

- *Lady palm - Rhapis excelsa*

- *Bamboo palm - Chamaedorea seifrizii*

- *Rubber plant - Ficus robusta or Ficus elastica*

- *Dracaena Janet Craig*

- *English ivy -Hedera helix*

- *Dwarf Date Palm - Phoenix roebelenii*

- *Ficus Macleilandii Alii*

- *Boston fern - Nephrolepis exaltata 'Bostoniensis'*

- *Peace lily - Spathiphyllum*

- *Dracaena fragrans 'Massangeana'*

- *Golden pothos - Epipremnum aureum*

- *Nephrolepis obliterata*
- *Gerbera jamesonii*
- *Dracaena deremensis*
- *Dracaena marginata*
- *Philodendron Erubescens*
- *Syngonium podophyllum*
- *Dieffenbachia "Exotica Compacta"*
- *Parlor Palm – Chamaedorea elegans*
- *Ficus benjamin*
- *Schefflera arboricola*
- *Begonia Semperflorens*
- *Philodendron selloum*
- *Philodendron oxycardium*
- *Sansevieria trifasciata*
- *Dieffenbachia "Camilla"*
- *Philodendron domesitcum*
- *Hamalomena wallisii*

- *Maranta leuconeura*
- *Christmas Cactus – Schlumbergera buckleyi*
- *Easter Cactus – Schlumbergera gaertneri*
- *Spider plant – Chlorophytum comosum*
- *Aglaonema crispum*
- *Croton – Codiaeum veriegatum pictum*
- *Dwarf Azalea – Rhodedendron simsii "Compacta"*
- *Calathea makoyana*
- *Aloe Vera – Aloe barbadensis*
- *Cereus Peruvianus*
- *Consolea facata*
- *Cassula argentea*
- *Tillandsia Cyanea*

Mother Nature offers us the most advanced and effective technology to reduce pollution and electromagnetic waves, and there are other benefits to having plants in our rooms. It was also noted that having opportunities to gaze intentionally at nearby plants on a daily basis in the work environment can reduce the psychological and physiological stress (Toyoda et al. 2020).

Finally, to conclude this look at the empowering environment, remember that you don't work on a desert island. Every day you have interactions with other **people that affect you.** These people impact your mindset, your health, and your productivity. Don't underestimate the power of the people around you. As Jim Rohn taught us, *"You are the average of the five people you spend the most time with"*.

The people around you are more important than you think. We all know the sayings, *"He who walks with the lame learns how to limp!"* or *"Tell me who you walk with, and I'll tell you who you are"*.

When you hang out with certain people or work with them, you will inevitably take on some of their mindset and personality traits.

Friends, family, and colleagues who are not generally positive will infect you with their negativity. The mindset is contagious; it spreads easily.

Surround yourself with the right people. Get close to people who support your goals and push away those who don't. You should surround yourself with people who don't take away your power, but who energize you. You should surround yourself with people who can encourage and assist you. Being with people who are thinking about success creates what researchers call a "positive success spiral" that lifts you up and gives you momentum (Keller, 2018).

Create a productivity-oriented environment that supports your life mission; remember that you never win or lose alone. That's why it's important to have a mastermind group and a good team. But we'll find that out in a bit...

3. The Importance of Collaboration

Although the first stage of success occurs initially in our minds through our capacity for imagination, it then becomes a matter of skill and ability to collaborate and cooperate with others. Success can be attributed to many things but essential factors lie in the skills and communication of those around you. The cliche "no man is an island" rings true due to the fact that you need other people to get things done. This is especially true of companies; they usually have projects that require collaboration from many employees thus forming teams. The importance of collaboration cannot be underestimated; it is an essential tool in building strong projects.

Collaboration is active participation, a synergistic relationship between two or more entities working together to produce something better than what they could do alone. So, at its foundation collaboration can be defined as the working together of employees, and sometimes managers, toward a common goal. These goals can be projects that fit into the bigger picture of the company and form part of company objectives. It could also be collaborating in working toward company culture and the reputation that the company wishes to exude.

There is strength in unity and this is best manifested through collaboration within companies to reach objectives. Collaboration brings together employees with different perspectives, skills, ideas, and varying levels of creativity. Companies increasingly need the knowledge of various professionals, with very different specializations, who work well as a team and collaborate effectively with each other to get a better overview.

> "In the long history of humankind (and animal kind, too) those who learned to collaborate and improvise most effectively have prevailed."
>
> Charles Darwin

Human resources are essential for problems because while many processes may be automated, employees have the ideas that drive what automation makes consistent. This form of problem-solving is what defines a company as strong, it hints at a good work culture that is diverse and respectful and has the ability to produce the best possible outcomes.

Collaboration is the basis of all work processes and ensures that a common goal is being worked towards. While having the best and most up-to-date technologies is helpful to a company, the foundation of good work remains the sharing of ideas and skills among employees. Additionally, it helps employees find their roles within a company. This is done through the setting of a common goal and a team working on it. Employees are then able to determine their best skills and this allows them to reach peak productivity when working with other people of varying skill sets.

The success of a company often lies in the ability of employees to collaborate as well as the plans of management to facilitate and allow for collaboration to grow and develop. In order for a company to develop and become a leader in its field it must prioritize collaboration. Whether the company is using a remote or smart working model, communication and the ability to work toward a common goal is what will define a company. Innovative, fresh, and new ideas are often borne of collaboration. The bringing together of new and creative skills and ideas in an environment that is safe, comfortable, and encouraging will lead to the company's objectives being realized.

The best performing teams are those that collaborate and work together in the best way, where all members are involved and actively participate in the project. All winning teams have winning collaborations.

Fig. 5: Collaboration leads to skill-sharing and efficiency.

Benefits of Collaboration

As mentioned above, collaboration is essential in achieving company goals. However, there are added benefits to collaboration aside from the completion of projects and the realization of objectives. Let's explore these, starting with an improved **sense of flexibility**. When teams and employees collaborate more often they begin to form a familiarity that solidifies relationships. This allows them to reach goals quicker and with more ease. The benefit of this is that when a company has to introduce something new or make changes, employees already have a sense of flexibility and will roll with the punches. The second benefit of collaboration is increased **engagement**. When employees begin to work together more frequently they are engaging with others, new ideas, and different skills. This improves the overall productivity of a company and ensures that employees are not stagnant, not achieving work satisfaction, and ultimately failing to reach company objectives.

A **company's productivity** also increases because collaboration allows the workload to be divided among its members. This reduces the pressure on the individual and ensures that the goal is achieved faster.

Another great benefit is that **problem-solving** becomes more effective and efficient because we have the opportunity to compare our ideas with others. When we combine different brains with different skills and expertise, we are better equipped to solve problems. This union of brains also helps us develop new points of view and have a broader view of reality. We are thus better able to know what needs to be accomplished and why. This phenomenon is amplified when we have a very heterogeneous team (different ages, genders, backgrounds, and nationalities) because it means listening to different opinions on a topic. The problem won't just be approached from one angle, and the team will be able to see a bigger picture.

Collaboration also promotes the **transfer of learning**. By working in a team, you have the opportunity to learn from the experiences of other group members and this favors the acquisition of new skills. Everyone in a group learns something new from others. Everyone has knowledge that others don't have.

Lastly, collaboration ensures that meetings are more fruitful and this is due to the collaborative culture. This means meetings are shorter and more informative as employees are more willing to complete their tasks due to working with others to realize their goals.

Collaboration Tips

Introducing collaboration can take some time and requires a plan to be successful. Here are some tips to make collaboration successful in your company. Collaboration should begin in the workplace using a **top-down approach**. This means that collaboration must begin with executives and managers working together in teams to reach goals so that they'll become ingrained in the company culture. By using executives and managers to realize core company values and goals, employees will begin to adopt collaboration as well, making them more efficient and effective at completing objectives. Additionally, this will improve engagement as authority figures within a company are exhibiting what is desirable to the company and employees will aim to use collaboration first.

Another practice that will make collaboration better is a **reward and incentives plan**. Aside from individual rewards and incentives that are usually motivating factors toward reaching a company objective, companies should adopt incentives for teams as well. This will encourage collaboration as not only are employees receiving bonuses but they are doing so due to effective and efficient work completion. This will also build good relationships among coworkers rather than rivalry.

To ensure that collaboration becomes a part of the company culture a good and clear guideline must be instated. **Clear communication** is key in getting employees to understand why they need to collaborate. Communication will too provide a clear path on how to use collaboration to achieve goals and objectives.

Having **effective communication** is important in other ways as well. It fosters knowledge sharing, resolves misunderstandings, and helps keep the team close-knit. When you develop and foster communication and empathy among members, you develop a collaborative spirit that creates an environment conducive to constructive exchange and discussion. A climate of trust is created, where people work in harmony towards the achievement of a common goal, where even the less extroverted are able to express themselves and give their contribution.

Effective collaboration between people can be facilitated by **technology**. There are many tools, and the advice is to choose tools that are simple and intuitive. Avoid software with a myriad of features that only distracts from the really important goals. Try to have tools that can interact with different platforms, for example Linux, Windows, Apple, iOS and Android. It can also be helpful to have cloud-based solutions so you can access the same information we can access in the office. But beware of privacy! Keep in mind that you are sharing valuable information with other companies.

Last, but not least, it is necessary to continuously **change and update** how a company uses collaboration. This will allow employees to effectively work with each other at every level and lead to more skill sharing amongst members of various teams. Using feedback from employees, managers and executives must make decisions that will make collaboration easier. Adapting is also necessary so that it allows the company to innovate.

Harnessing the Web for International Collaboration

Types of Collaboration

Before we can dive into what using the web for international collaboration is about, let's first define the types of collaboration you get. The first type of collaboration is **team collaboration**. A collaborative team is a group that collaborates that not only works together, but also shares responsibilities. They work together, think together, reason together. One member can complete another's work if the other is struggling. Usually there is no real leader, rather it is shared leadership (people within a team lead each other), although in some cases temporary leaders emerge based on the task. When an important member is absent, the collaborative team still manages to complete the task.

Team collaboration should not be misunderstood with teamwork. In both cases, people work together to complete a shared goal, but the key difference is that while teamwork combines the individual efforts of all team members to achieve a goal, people working collaboratively complete a project collectively (Civil Service College, 2018).

A group of people working together as a team is working on an individual level. Each team member has a task to perform and a specific role that contributes to the overall goal.

This is wherein there is a predetermined team of people with a fixed set of goals and deadlines. The purpose of this type of collaboration is to get people to work independently within a time frame thereby achieving the larger goal that had been set out for the team. This can be illustrated with an example of a marketing department of ten people, each person has a particular role in the team and when all tasks are successfully completed the end product is a marketing campaign for the company product. Communication is key for this type of collaboration as members must clearly understand their tasks for the overall objective to be reached. The example of sports teams can also be given. They all have the same overall goal, but they also have specific roles and jobs (and there is well-defined leadership).

The second type of collaboration is referred to as **community collaboration.** The goal is to bring individuals, agencies, organizations, community members in an atmosphere of support to systematically solve existing and emerging problems that could not easily be solved by one group alone. The end goal of this type of collaboration is to learn rather than to have a completed task. This type does not have a fixed deadline and is an ongoing and ever-changing process wherein members learn problem-solving. This ensures that members can use what they've learned in other aspects of their work and thereby boosting their productivity. Is a process where stakeholders work together to share information and resources in order to fulfill a shared vision and goals.

The third type of collaboration is **collaboration network** (also known as a collaborative network or CN). Is a network consisting of a variety of entities (e.g. organizations, people, machines) that are largely autonomous, geographically distributed, and heterogeneous in terms of their operating environment, culture, social capital and goals, but that collaborate to better achieve common or compatible goals, thus jointly generating value, and whose interactions are supported by computer network.

CN actors are aware that together, the network members can achieve goals that would not be possible or would have a higher cost if attempted by them individually. Camarinha-Matos — university professor expert in collaborative networks, and virtual enterprises and organizations — tells us that an **Innovation Ecosystem** (IE) is also a CN, as it is formed by autonomous, independent, distributed and heterogeneous actors that behave, interact and collaborate with each other with different roles in a socio-technical network within a fertile, spatial and evolving environment to overcome individual capability limitations, maximize the use of resources, and share risks and costs, so as better achieve common/compatible goals regarding the different involved cultures and intrinsic network dynamics (Camarinha-Matos et al., 2015).

Innovation ecosystem is the term used to describe the large number and diverse nature of participants and resources that are necessary for innovation. These include "entrepreneurs, investors, researchers, university faculty, venture capitalists as well as business development and other technical service providers such as accountants, designers, contract manufacturers and providers of skills training and professional development (Jackson, 2011). An IE is not always created as a methodologically planned and induced initiative of some actors. There are several case (e.g. Silicon Valley) with have simply emerged as a result of a set of regional factors (Camarinha-Matos et al., 2015).

We can identify other different forms of CN, some of them can be quite complex. Thanks to new opportunities and the vast amount of information that the Web offers us, these networks have evolved over time.

Virtual Organization (VO): is a temporary consortium of partners from different organizations established to fulfil a value adding task, for example a product or service to a customer (Kürümlüoglu et al., 2005). This type of organization does not have a physical infrastructure, uses technology to collaborate, and is a loose alliance of professionals or companies (Simon, 2017).

Dynamic Virtual Organization (DVO): When a short-term Business Opportunity (BO) occurs, fast configuration of a temporary consortium, which appropriate to its needs will be formed. This consortium is so-called Dynamic Virtual Organization, which represents a temporary alliance of different organizations that sharing knowledge, skills, and resources in order to respond to achieve the specific Business Opportunity. DVOs often dissolve when they reach their goal (Yassa et al., 2014).

Virtual Enterprise (VE): is a particular case of a VO. Is a formalized collaboration between two or more autonomous organizations for the achievement of a specific business goal. They often begin with investments and a sharing of overhead. Once the project is complete these entities often separate. The paradigm of virtual enterprise represents a major area of research and technological development for industrial enterprises and an important application area for web-based cooperative environments. We can say that the VE concept is one of the most important ways to raise the agility and competitiveness of manufacturing enterprises (Angulo et al., n.d.).

We can identified two well-defined categories of VE, namely the *Static Virtual Enterprise (SVE)* where the network is fixed and predetermined — business and commercial processes, and business relationships are predefined, fixed, integrated and static — and the *Dynamic Virtual Enterprise (DVE)* where the network is dynamic — business partners change according to market needs and are selected through negotiation (Ouzounis, 2001).

Extended Enterprise (EE): An extended enterprise is a loosely coupled, self-organizing network of firms that combine their economic output to provide products and services offerings to the market and pursue repeated, enduring exchange relations with one another.

Professional Virtual Community (PVC): PVCs represent both professional and virtual communities. Acting as an environment for collaboration and sharing, they provide a sense of community for professionals who are spread across the globe (Simon, 2017). The combination of virtual community and professional community concepts. Virtual communities are defined as social systems of networks of individuals who use computer technologies to mediate their relationships. Professional communities provide environments for professionals to share the body of knowledge of their professions such as similar working cultures, problem perceptions, problem-solving techniques, professional values, and behavior (Camarinha-Matos &

Afsarmanesh, 2005).

Virtual Manufacturing Network (VMN): A Virtual Manufacturing Network is a manufacturing network which is not owned by a simple company, but it is built with the use of ICT for bringing together different suppliers and alliance partners creating in such a way a virtual network which is able to operate as a solely owned supply network. Using information and communications technology (ICT), a VMN brings together different suppliers and partners. The VMN manages the configuration, management, and monitoring of the manufacturing process through technology (Simon, 2017).

The "Virtual Manufacturing" can enhance one or several levels of decision and control in manufacturing process (Product and Process Design, Process and Production Planning, Machine Tool, Robot and Manufacturing System). As automation technologies such as CAD/CAM have sped up product design, Virtual Manufacturing will have a similar effect on the manufacturing phase thanks to the modelling, simulation and optimization of the product and the processes involved in its fabrication (Dépincé et al., 2004).

Agile Shop Floor: In the manufacturing industry, the agile shop floor is a collaboration network that enables rapid change. Different cells of the shop floor involved in the manufacturing process make themselves readily available by contract (Simon, 2017). The dynamic environment of a virtual enterprise requires that partners in the consortium own reconfigurable shop floors (Ribeiro & Barata, 2006). This is a promising approach to allow rapid changes in the shop-floor infrastructure and its control system (Camarinha-Matos, 2004).

E-Science: This type of global collaborative community is specific to science and enables the sharing of resources between professionals and institutions. It also involves ICT infrastructure that enables flexible, secure, and coordinated sharing of resources. Wikis, blogs, virtual social networks, grid computing and open access are just a brief selection of related new technologies. Right now, no generally used term or common definition of e-science exists, which limits the understanding of the true potential of the concept (Koschtial, 2021).

It can be defined as a scientific collaboration network (SCN) or scholarly collaboration network or social sharing network. Scientists first used this type of collaboration network to share research and publications with one another. They are also used by academics as social networking sites. Within the last few years, however, scientists have been able to organize international collaborations to further research progress (Simon, 2017).

Virtual Laboratory: This type of e-Science environment represents a heterogeneous and distributed problem solving environment that allows scientists and researchers scattered in different centers around the globe to share resources such as data, information, equipment and tools.

Similar to Innovation Ecosystems – due to their long-term alliance nature – we encounter *Business Ecosystem* and VO *Breeding Environment (VBE)*.

Business Ecosystem: A collection of organizations involved in the development and delivery of a specific product or service through simultaneous competition and cooperation. This network can consist of suppliers, customers, and regulatory agencies. (They are similar to business clusters: a geographic concentration of interconnected businesses, suppliers, and associated institutions in a particular field. Clusters are considered to increase the productivity with which companies can compete, nationally and globally). An IE is a broader concept and is more open and dynamically emerging environment than a Business Ecosystem.

VO Breeding Environment (VBE): An association (also known as cluster) or pool of organizations and their related supporting institutions that have both the potential and the will to cooperate with each other through the establishment of a "base" long-term cooperation agreement and interoperable infrastructure (Camarinha-Matos & Afsarmanesh, 2005) and adoption of common operating principles and infrastructures, with the main goal of increasing both their chances and their preparedness towards collaboration in potential Virtual Organizations (Afsarmanesh & Camarinha-Matos, 2005).

These organizations make themselves available for opportunities. Acting as a broker, one member chooses which businesses make sense for the project and then contracts them. Upon entry to the VBE, members set up the infrastructure and agreements (Simon, 2017). So, is a regulated open, but controlled-border association of its members. It aims at improving the preparedness of its member organizations for joining potential future VOs, hence providing a cradle for dynamic and agile establishment of opportunity-driven collaborative networks. (Afsarmanesh & Camarinha-Matos, 2005).

VBEs motivate the creation of Virtual Organizations (VO) as organizations that respond with high flexibility to rapid changes in market needs. VBEs define (implicit or explicit) main working and sharing principles in order to impulse collaboration between members and assure long-term benefits (Galeano Sánchez et al., n.d.).

To attract and maintain members and partners, it is

important to define a system of incentives. Incentives can be knowledge and business benefits: cost benefits, guaranteed participation in a given number of VOs, tutorials and courses to improve business skills (such as productivity), and member support with constructive suggestions and advice.

Now that you have a clearer view on collaborative networks, you'll find it helpful to know that an Innovation Ecosystem typically embraces many kinds of actors, existing infrastructures and even other collaborative networks. Because there is no physical or organizational border, IEs embrace university, private R&D lavs, funding agencies and banks, etc., besides previously established industrial clusters, innovation habitats and VBEs. Therefore, IEs can be considered as a "logical" environment on top of existing CN and other non-CNs alliances (Camarinha-Matos et al., 2015). Finally, Innovation Ecosystems can interact with other IEs.

Collaborative networks are today applied in a wide variety of sectors, including industrial production, services, logistics and transport, scientific research, development, energy management, education, agribusiness, government, elderly care, and more.

As you can see, collaboration can do wonders for you. The potential benefits of collaboration are endless. We've seen how companies can develop collaborative networks with complementary organizations or professionals to be competitive in certain businesses, markets, or scientific innovations.

Collaborative networks play a relevant role in the establishment of new socio-economic and organizational structures; represent a highly promising approach for value co-creation and an important mechanism to help organizations better respond to business opportunities or survive in turbulent and uncertain conditions (Camarinha-Matos, 2009).

How to Grow and Interact with Network Collaboration

As explained above network collaboration is ever-changing and has recently become more popular with the growth of businesses due to the new problems that businesses and society face. A large part of this can be traced back to the lowering of consumer barriers and the increase of the pool of goods and services that consumers are now able to indulge in. This level of access demanded better quality of goods and services through diversity and thus network collaboration was necessary. Information and technology needed to evolve so that it would meet the consumer market and this was only possible through virtual businesses and the formation of network collaboration through the virtual world. A benefit to your company using network collaboration is that the business becomes stronger. That is, they are able to overcome any challenges or volatility that the market may be going through due to their increased access to information that expands not only their market but their knowledge base as well.

In addition to this, network collaboration allows companies to have a better understanding of the market and what the company hopes to achieve. This ensures that a company is not only focusing on reaching their objectives but also on growing and developing the market within which they operate. The innovation that it is able to create forms a new type of value, or creation of value, therefore expanding the base of knowledge with which the market is run. Network collaboration focuses on the knowledge, skills, subjectivity of those involved, and the external factors that may objectively affect all those involved.

The creation of network collaboration is often done through virtual businesses and thus the internet plays an important role. The internet has the ability to connect people in various locations, with various identities, skills, and knowledge. This not only allows network collaboration to be better developed than regular collaboration but also leaves room for an element of diversity to grow and develop thereby expanding the knowledge and reach that a company may have because collaborative networks are complex systems needing multi-disciplinary contributions and a combination of different perspectives.

Network collaboration, while having the potential to form these large and diverse knowledge-filled bases, may run into the issue of not being able to assign which member may be providing the value to a product or the knowledge base. When teams are spread across various geographic locations and work on different hours and with varying methods, it is not easy to understand where exactly the value that the company is creating may be coming from. This could mean that there are gaps in particular markets that may not be contributing as much. These gaps could affect an intangible knowledge collection base and have the potential to be missed when translating knowledge into the added value that goes into a better quality product.

To ensure that the company is able to use network collaboration to its best potential there are three factors that build network collaboration. Namely, they are *networking*, *coordination*, and *cooperation*. To understand how they form part of successful collaboration they will be defined.

Networking can be defined as the ability to create contacts to expand opportunities and to share information through communication for a shared benefit.

Coordination is the unification, integration,

synchronization of the efforts of group members so as to provide unity of action in the pursuit of common goals. So, unity of action among the employees, groups, and departments, but it is also the ability of management to assign how and when particular tasks must be met so that even though team members are working from various time zones they are able to fulfill their assigned work.

Cooperation is in opposition to working in competition for selfish benefit. It is the process of groups of organisms working or acting together for a common and mutual benefit. It is the ability to share resources in addition to information thereby increasing the potential for work to be done efficiently and effectively by the team. So, people helping each other out to achieve a common goal and have mutual benefits.

Using these ideas and the power of the internet network collaboration will allow your company to soar.

Where can you start to build your collaborative network and thus have a competitive advantage in the marketplace? Start by setting up your network of experts, partners, customers and suppliers. Start by creating a mastermind group with them and lay the groundwork for a medium- to long-term strategic alliance. If they don't know what you're talking about, you can give them this book as a gift. If you learn to join forces, you will become unstoppable.

This way, you acquire a variety of benefits, including co-creating goods and services, shifting to the shared value and culture of collaboration, moving your industry toward its goals, creating flexibility in your workplace, making use of technology and cultivating a tech-savvy workforce, creating sustainable businesses, and getting employees trained quickly.

You'll gain a range of benefits, including co-creating goods and services, creating sustainable businesses, cultivating a tech-savvy workforce, and having access to much broader, multidisciplinary knowledge.

Current developments in ICT, namely ubiquitous computing and networking, offer possibilities to interlink competencies and resources, lowering the dependency on geographical barriers, which represents an opportunity to fight chronic regional unbalances (Camarinha-Matos, 2009). Even as you become more collaborative, significant challenges will remain. Like optimal network configuration and finding the right partners, not just those that are available to participate. The biggest challenge lies in security. Keeping information secret in a technological world is almost a utopia. But participation in networks has become very important for any organization that strives to achieve a competitive advantage in turbulent market conditions, especially in the case of small and medium sized enterprises.

Regarding security, Maxim Sytch — a researcher with the University of Michigan's Ross School of Business — found that most open networks that form research and development agreements with partners from different industries and geographies, are usually less secure with company secrets, but evolves faster (this is the example of more technologically dynamic industries such as biotechnology and microelectronics). While more closed networks that only forge collaborations with known or recommended partners limit overall progress, but manage to keep company secrets secure (chemical, pharmaceutical, and automotive industries).

Fig. 6: Network collaboration allows companies to have employees anywhere in the world.

How to Use Smart and Remote Working with Network Collaboration

As illustrated above, network collaboration can be a priceless asset in building a strong and efficient company. Network collaboration relies on the technologies that make smart work possible as well as the model of remote work to ensure that work is of high quality and completed timeously. Network collaboration can be easily integrated into a model of remote or smart working through clear communication and guided schedules of task completion.

That being said, I think a few issues need to be addressed now to avoid running into serious problems and hurting the company's communication and productivity.

A team of researchers (Longqi Yang, David Holtz, Sonia Jaffe, Siddharth Suri, Shilpi Sinha, Jeffrey Weston, Connor Joyce, Neha Shah, Kevin Sherman, Brent Hecht and Jaime Teevan) who analyzed rich data on the emails, calendars, instant messages, video/audio calls and workweek hours of 61,182 US Microsoft employees over the first six months of 2020 to estimate the causal effects of firm-wide remote work on collaboration and communication found that firm-wide remote work caused the collaboration network of workers to become more static and siloed, with fewer bridges between disparate parts. Furthermore, there was a decrease in synchronous communication and an increase in asynchronous communication. Together, these effects may make it harder for employees to acquire and share new information across the network (L Yang et al., 2021).

Is remote working really impeding collaboration and communication? We know that the shift to remote work has had a significant impact on workplace communication and collaboration between workers.

Microsoft's company-wide shift to remote work has hurt communication and collaboration among different business groups inside the company, threatening employee productivity and long-term innovation (Roe, 2021).

The study found that fully remote workers spent 25% less time collaborating, had fewer real-time conversations, and decreased hours spent in meetings by 5% (Kekatos, 2021).

The report published in Nature Human Behaviour states:

"Our results show that the shift to firm-wide remote work caused business groups within Microsoft to become less interconnected. It also reduced the number of ties bridging structural holes in the company's informal collaboration network and caused individuals to spend less time collaborating with the bridging ties that remained."[6]

6. A network-bridging tie is a relationship that spans a structural hole in a network, i.e., it is defined by the network structure that surrounds the tie, and it can be either a strong or weak tie (Levin, 2011). Bridging ties are important for obtaining new information. However, when entrepreneurs try

to bridge between two networks, they may face problems due to the variety of knowledge among individuals in both networks (Scholten et al. 2015).

"Furthermore, the shift to firm-wide remote work caused employees to spend a greater share of their collaboration time with their stronger ties, which are better suited to information transfer, and a smaller share of their time with weak ties, which are more likely to provide access to new information."

"We expect that the effects we observe on workers' collaboration and communication patterns will impact productivity and, in the long-term, innovation. Yet, across many sectors, firms are making decisions to adopt permanent remote work policies based only on short-term data."

"Firms making decisions on the basis of non-causal analyses may set suboptimal policies. For example, some firms that choose a permanent remote work policy may put themselves at a disadvantage by making it more difficult for workers to collaborate and exchange information."

"Beyond estimating the causal effects of firm-wide remote work, our results also provide preliminary insights into the effects of remote work policies such as mixed-mode and hybrid work. Specifically, the non-trivial collaborator effects that we estimate suggest that hybrid and mixed-mode work arrangements may not work as firms expect. The most effective implementations of hybrid and mixed-mode work might be those that deliberately attempt to minimize the impact of collaborator effects on those employees that are not working remotely; for example, firms might consider implementations of hybrid work in which certain teams come into the office on certain days, or in which most or all workers come into the office on some days and work remotely otherwise."

Regarding hybrid solutions, Professor David Holtz, co-author of this study, tell us that "The fact that your colleagues' remote work status affects your own work habits has major implications for companies that are considering hybrid or mixed-mode work policies," he said. For example, having one's teammates and collaborators in the office at the same time improves communication and information flow for both those in and out of the office. "It's important to be thoughtful about how these policies are implemented"(Barkley, 2021).

Vadim Tabakman — vice president, global presales at Nintex — points out that it is possible to find areas of any business where Microsoft's claims are correct or incorrect, and it all depends on the technology and resources that employees have at their disposal (Roe, 2021). I would also add that these dynamics depend on the number of people involved. The study in question involves 61,182 employees, not a group of 10 or 50 people.

Amie Devero — an executive coach and strategy consultant to tech companies — meetings have continued in companies with remote working, speaking from her experience tells us that team meetings and one-on-ones have continued in companies with remote working, but that lateral and diagonal communication between members of different teams, between managers with team-members of other teams, between tenured and new employees in different functions has largely stopped (Roe, 2021). She tell us that "Individual teams communicate within themselves. They craft their own strategies and tactics, not to mention cultivating their own cultures."

"That erodes the grand vision of one strategy and one mission. So disparate teams have little experience or knowledge about other teams except through scorecards or dashboards. Relationships don't form or get fostered. Innovation exists in a smaller setting with fewer interconnections. Since innovation depends on connections made between unlike or even unlikely things, it is, by definition, limited" (Roe, 2021).

This is really very useful and valuable information; the smaller and more slender settings will perhaps smile. Those who opt for hybrid or mixed solutions will also appreciate this information.

Hybrid solutions solve a potential problem with new hires working remotely. New hires do not know their colleagues and have never spent time in the office like other older colleagues (Niu, 2021). As a result, newcomers don't get to "live the culture of the company." This translates into being 20% less likely to acknowledge company values (Hyken,

2021).

Rolf Bax — Chief Human Resources Officer of Resume.io — gives us more valuable information: "I've also found it more difficult to successfully orient new hires to their role remotely, I think the biggest challenge of remote onboarding compared to traditional in-person methods is that it is more difficult for a new hire to get a feel for an organization's culture and its people from behind a screen."

Onboarding (or organizational socialization) refers to an integration process; the post-hiring process that involves the bringing the new resource into the enterprise. It is a practice to accelerate the integration of human resources that include initiatives to improve the entry of newcomers.

To conclude this look at how to use remote and smart working in the best possible way, we will now shed more light on **communication styles.**

From the research conducted on Microsoft employees, we saw how remote work caused workers to spend more time using asynchronous forms of communication, such as email and message platforms, and less time having synchronous conversations in person, by phone, or by video conference (Barkley, 2021).

To better understand what happened, some terms will be defined now.

Asynchronous communication: communication that occurs not in real time. Response times are variable and doesn't require the recipient's immediate attention. Example: email, online forums, collaborative documents, social networks, chat, messaging applications. Everyone has the opportunity to communicate at their own preferred times. The sender sends their message and engages in other activities.

Synchronous communication: communications happen in real time. Example: live communication, telephone, video call. Immediate attention of the recipient is required. We can also use chat and messaging applications, but in this case, there may be small delays in response (receiving the message, reading, deciphering, thinking and writing the response).

There can also be a **hybrid mode of communication** using chat and messaging applications. These applications allow for asynchronous communication when those involved are not simultaneously connected, and synchronous communication when they are online.

It becomes critical to business communication and productivity to understand when to use one mode rather than the other to exchange information. This is a skill that can increase the efficiency of any work group. The team should not waste time and energy.

Managers will need to promote:

- *The use of synchronous communication in the face of situations of uncertainty. Example: a member does not know how to move on a particular task and needs information to proceed. If the information is delayed, his productivity is hampered.*

- *The transition from asynchronous to synchronous communication in the face of misunderstandings. For example, if there is little understanding during an email or chat message exchange, avoid prolonging the conversation, and clarify verbally.*

- *The use of email when we need to give detailed, accurate and comprehensive responses.*

- *The brief use of chats. Chats need to speed up and simplify communication. A 30-minute exchange of information in chat is a waste of time. It could have been done in 10 minutes with a switch to synchronous communication.*

- *The preference of synchronous communication in the face of unclear and chaotic situations, and also those that are urgent and emergency.*

Therefore, they will have to discourage:

- *Sending too many emails on the same topic and having long chats when you see a lack of understanding.*

- *The solicitation of responses through an asynchronous tool in the face of urgent situations unless the urgency is well evidenced.*

- *Sending unclear and confusing written communications. In these cases, it's best to talk to each other verbally for clarification.*

The full understanding of the dynamics faced so far will give you a major competitive advantage. The information you have received will be critical to the performance, efficiency and productivity of your business.

The Traps of Virtual Reality

When we move through an environment, we need to know the characteristics of the environment in which we move. It is important to understand the characteristics and operation of virtual environments.

These are often environments where **siloed communication** is formed. Because social networks want you to spend as much time as possible on their platforms, they use many strategies. Social network algorithms make people relate to like-minded people with similar values and ideals and related interests. Algorithms limit the encounter with diversity, you will hardly be suggested pages or profiles that are not in line with your interests, otherwise they risk losing your attention, which means losing profits.

In these environments there is often a tendency to **conform to one's peers**, where people within a group rather than saying what they really think, say things that can be shared and approved by other members. The tragedy is that it seems that for many, the important thing is to please others, to receive likes and shares, rather than to truly be oneself; to express and manifest one's true essence.

In addition to this, it is useful to remember that the majority of **data traffic on the web** belongs to only a very few global players.

4. The Mastermind Group

I have already written a book devoted to mastermind groups, discussing the historical origins, creation, and management of the mastermind group.[7] Therefore, what I will attempt to do in this chapter is to approach the topic from other angles.

[7]. *The Power of the Mastermind Group* is a small but fundamental book for anyone who wants to understand how a mastermind group works and how to manage and create one. On my YouTube channel "Edoardo Zeloni Magelli" you can listen to most of the audiobook for free. I take this opportunity to invite you to subscribe to my social channels not to miss other valuable information and to download the free resources for the mind that you can find on zelonimagelli.com.

Since there are almost infinite nuances when it comes to Mastermind Groups, I feel it is appropriate to define it in new terms, and more congruent with the theme of the book. Aware of the fact, that in other contexts, I would write this chapter on mastermind groups in other ways and with other content. It would be a completely different chapter, but equally correct to define a mastermind group.

> "The Mastermind principle consists of an alliance of two or more minds working in perfect harmony for the attainment of a common definite objective. Success does not come without the cooperation of others"
>
> Napoleon Hill

The Master Mind

Napoleon Hill coined the term "master mind alliance", also known as "brain alliance", and defined this to be the harmonious working between two or more people toward a particular end. The term has since been modernized and is now called the mastermind group. The mastermind group as explained by Hill is the collaboration of effort and knowledge between two or more people who are working toward a defined goal, he further explains that two minds cannot work together without the formation of an invisible third mind (an intangible force), which may be referred to as the master mind.

"No two minds ever come together without, thereby, creating a third, invisible, intangible force which may be likened to a third mind."

Napoleon Hill

The Chemistry of the Mind

The mastermind principle finds its foundation in natural laws. Each human brain is a transmitting and broadcasting station; both of emission and reception for the vibrations of the frequency of thought.

Every mind is directly connected with every other mind through the ether. Any thought released by any mind, can be immediately picked up and interpreted by other minds.

Some minds when they come into contact show a natural affinity for each other, while others show a strong dislike. In between these two extremes there are many other possibilities for reactions. Sometimes these results occur without having uttered a single word.

We are vibrating energy, and our mind is made up of a mental substance that causes a chemical reaction when it comes into contact with other mental substances from other minds. This chemical reaction creates vibrations that can be pleasant or unpleasant. With some people we feel very good, with others less; the effect of the union of two minds is evident: a completely different state of mind is provoked from the one that existed just before the interaction. When two minds come into contact with each other, a remarkable change takes place in both. The mental substances that have come into contact, have generated a new energy field that has changed the mood.

Each mind has its own energy field that we can call the **mental electric field**. The mental electric field is constantly changing, and is influenced by the chemistry of the mind, which is changeable.[8]

[8]. The human body produces an electromagnetic field. We are electromagnetic. Each of our cells produces an electromagnetic field. Life is based on two aspects: matter and a non-material, electrical component (Fels, 2018).

Advances in biophysics, biology, functional genomics, neuroscience, psychology, psychoneuroimmunology, and other fields suggest the existence of a subtle system of "biofield" interactions that organize biological processes from the subatomic, atomic, molecular, cellular, and organismic to the interpersonal and cosmic levels (Muehsam et al. 2015).

The biofield or biological field, is a complex organizing energy field engaged in the generation, maintenance, and regulation of biological homeodynamics (Rubik et al., 2015). The properties of such a field could be based on electromagnetic fields, coherent states, biophotons, quantum and quantum-like processes, and ultimately the quantum vacuum (Kafatos et al., 2015). The human aura is an example of one familiar type of biofield that has gained acceptance in scientific circles as laboratory studies have correlated aura readers' observations with measurable changes in electromagnetic signals emanating from the person whose aura is being read (Dean, 2003).

The biofield is a large field of energy that surrounds and extends out from the body, approximately it is 5 feet to both sides and 3 feet above and below (McKusick, 2014). The mental electric field has a greater extent and can vary from person to person. A mental electric field can communicate with another field on the other side of the world. We are able to access information of all kinds through electrical impulses.

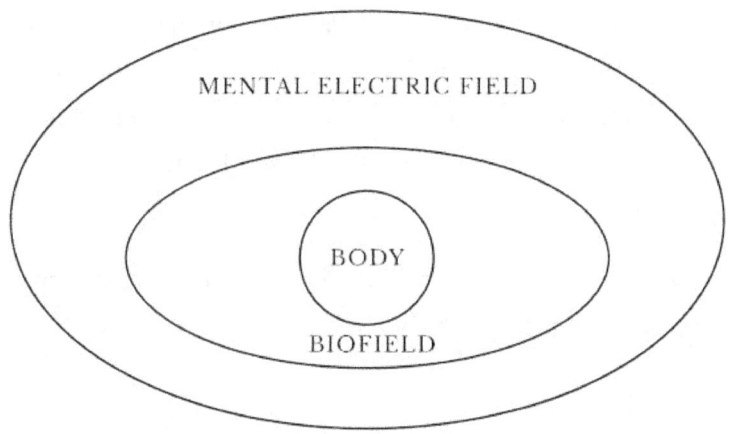

Fig. 7: Body, Biofield and Mental Electric Field.

Biofield interactions may bring about regulation of biochemical, cellular, and neurological processes through means related to electromagnetism, quantum fields, and perhaps other means of modulating biological activity and information flow (Muehsam et al. 2015).

In the inner electrical environment of our bodies, the magic of life unfolds and this environment is also able to be influenced in a powerful manner through sound vibrations (McKusick, 2014) and the vibrations of other minds.

The nature of this field varies according to the energetic frequency of the individual mind and the chemical reactions caused by interactions with other minds.

This energy field is able to attract certain people, things, situations and events, and likewise is able to repel them. This process can occur without the aid of words, facial expressions, or other forms of bodily movement or behavior.

It's possible to chemically change one's mind to attract or repel other minds, to form a master mind.

The Perfect Harmony

Harmony is another law of nature that enables life. Life is energy organized in harmony. Harmony pervades every single atom of the health of nature, our bodies and our minds. When harmony fails, a process begins that leads to death. This is what happens in natural ecosystems and also in our bodies. When organs stop functioning in harmony, life is weakened.[9]

[9]. We will now look at how important harmony is to our bodies, and then understand the importance of harmony in our surroundings, as the energy fields of places and people, interact with our own and influence us. We are all interconnected.

Quantum mechanics has established the primacy of the unseparable whole. For this reason, the basis of the new biophysics must be the insight into the fundamental interconnectedness within the organism as well as between organisms, and that of the organism with the environment (Popp & Beloussov, 2013). Our cells produce a biological magnetic field that keeps us healthy. Every cell knows and talks to every other cell. Cells exchange thousands of bits of information per second and form a giant communication network. The body can be considered as a large quantum system, in which an important role is played by bio-communication between cells. This exchange of information makes it possible to regulate the shape, growth, and regeneration of the organism and presides over the interactions between body and mind (Centro di Medicina Biologica, 2019).

When cells hear information they can put themselves in balance or disequilibrium. Cell-to-cell communication is the basis of coordinated cellular activity and thus fundamental for the functioning of biological systems (Scholkmann et al., 2013). A dialogue in harmony between the electromagnetic level of living matter and the chemical level ensures that the traffic of molecules is well ordered. Most investigators define the biofield in terms of low-level but measurable electromagnetic activities that play as critical a role in maintaining health as do the more thoroughly studied chemical, biochemical, and bioelectrical phenomena that Western medicine typically addresses (Dean, 2003).

The biofield is the result of different energetic components such as electromagnetic, acoustic and vibrational waves of endogenous nature, therefore originating from our interior. The organism, therefore, can be depicted as a bio-informational and bio-cybernetic entity, in which energy vibrations are able to transfer information from one point to another of the body allowing the development, organization and health status (Centro di Medicina Biologica, 2019).

Electromagnetic alterations, are able to affect our organic functions and our vital energy (Bernardi, 2018). Vital processes are regulated by electromagnetic oscillations, in charge of biochemical processes, the disease can be seen as a set of "sick" oscillations that lead to incorrect adjustments: the disease before manifesting itself in body symptoms can be sought in a disturbance of physiological frequency oscillations, disturbance on which you can intervene through counter-regulation or empowerment (Lifegate, 2009).

Our health is affected by the functioning of our electromagnetic fields. We are a community of 100 trillion cells that get along with each other. When the magnetic field does not work in harmony we develop pathologies.

Dr. Franco Lenna — medical expert in homeopathy with holistic address and biophysical-quantum medicine — tells us that when our biological magnetic field is no longer effective, we develop the disease, the cells stop communicating through their electromagnetic language and the pathology begins (not the traumatic pathology that is a mechanical fact that affects only about 5% of diseases). By restoring the correct magnetic field, many pathologies go away. So it's a restoration of frequencies. Each organ has its own frequency. We need to put the various parameters of our cells back into balance. We must intervene on the totality, putting more order, more agreement and balance between the various cells.

When we restore the harmonic frequencies of our magnetic field many diseases disappear. Biofield is the primary locus of healing and that most forms of human disease and dysfunction are potentially susceptible to correction through the biofield (Dean, 2003).

Dr. Piergiorgio Spaggiari — physicist, physician and professor expert in Quantum Medicine — points out that a pathology can be treated through the correct use of a drug (biochemical aspect) or through bioresonance. That is the use of ultra-weak electromagnetic fields able to modify the electromagnetic field of disturbance which was followed by a wrong reaction (biophysical aspect). He also points out that underneath the electromagnetic, biochemical and neurological phenomena there is always quantum physics, which in the field of biology has brought the new concept of inter-connection between the various parts of the body, between organisms and between them and their environment.

We are interconnected with our environment. All these processes within the biofield are also influenced by the energy fields of the people around us, which is also why it is very important to surround ourselves with "empowering people" and remove the "depowering people". The energy of the people around us affects our health. Everything in the universe has a vibration. Our body is made up of organs that vibrate, the people around us vibrate on certain frequencies and have their own energy fields.

We cannot stay "tuned" for long by being in an environment with frequencies that are dissonant and not compatible with our own. We must stay in places and surround ourselves with people who enhance our frequencies, and harmonize them. For example, when we are with people we love, our organism receives harmonizing frequencies, and we feel good.

We must seek harmony in physical places and in our relationships with others, since electromagnetic fields influence our state of health and our body reacts to electromagnetic stimuli. As I teach in my Primordial Psychology courses, the future of a seed depends not only on its qualities, but also on its soil (physical place; family; partners; friends; colleagues; school; social, political, cultural and legislative aspects of a city).

A master mind can be formed through the grouping or union in a spirit of perfect harmony of two or more minds. From the harmonious fusion of two or more minds — thus from the chemical reaction of the mental substances involved — a superior, intangible force is created that we can compare to a third mind, which can be used and assimilated by one or all of the individual minds.

The harmonious cooperation of two or more people who ally themselves for the purpose of accomplishing a particular goal develop the presence of a supreme mind, which can guide, inspire, offer ideas and insights, and nurture one or all of the individual minds.

It may be difficult to understand this phenomenon at first because it is not perceived with the five senses, but there are higher intangible forces and we are all guided by invisible, intangible energies.

As Hill taught us, this master mind remains available as long as the friendly, harmonious alliance between individual minds endures; and it will disintegrate, and with it all evidence of its former existence, the moment this alliance breaks down. If the minds involved in this process begin to take divergent paths, the master mind will disintegrate.

Since the master mind is a force that arises from the fusion and coordination of two or more minds in a spirit of perfect harmony, there can be no development of a master mind if the element of perfect harmony is lacking.

In a spirit of harmony, the individual minds of a group of people can form a master mind; the chemistry of the individual minds is modified so that these minds merge and function as one mind.

The ways in which these blending and mixing processes occur are numerous and will not be addressed in this book.

Mastermind Groups

Hill states that the structure in which the mastermind group is created will determine its success. That is, there should be a clear leader (although there are instances where shared leadership is preferred), a goal to work toward, as well as regular meetings. These ideals will be expanded upon below.

Mastermind groups usually lay their foundations in the mutual and beneficial sharing of knowledge and resources between people. The idea of a mastermind group is that by sharing and taking from others each person is able to achieve their goals much quicker than if they had attempted to complete their tasks alone. Hill attributes large success to using mastermind groups. He explains that through these beneficial and harmonious contributions each party involved walks away with something of value. This could be monetary wealth or even simply knowledge gain. Mastermind groups are designed to be able to create an independence wherein those involved are eventually able to set their own working hours, determine their own prices, as well as be able to determine their income.

As they are currently practiced, mastermind groups are spaces that are led by facilitators that allow them to discuss, brainstorm, and problem-solve so that the people in these groups can improve their personal and business skills. Mastermind groups not only allow members to create goals that are clearly aligned with their values but encourage members to achieve these goals. Members are also encouraged to support each other in reaching one's goals, either business or personal or sometimes both. The process of a mastermind group begins with the creation of goals and then moves towards making a plan to achieve the goal. In addition to this success stories of those who have already been through the process are mentioned and strived toward so that current mastermind groups are inspired. The group is involved in creating your plan to achieve your goals, through brainstorming and the sharing of creative ideas, and this allows you to bring your own success story to the group and inspire others to reach their goals.

Fig. 8: Mastermind groups are usually composed of between two and eight people.

Now that mastermind groups have been expanded upon, this chapter will focus on how to create a mastermind group, the heterogeneity of mastermind groups, the benefits of these groups as well as the drawbacks, and how to create and manage a virtual mastermind group.

How to Create a Mastermind Group

Most people are good at working on their own to achieve their goals. However, when working with like-minded individuals, it's been found that goals are achieved much quicker. Hill expanded on this with the mastermind principle as explained above. It may seem like a daunting task to find like-minded individuals but starting a mastermind group is easier than you would think. To begin the creation of a mastermind group you have to **settle on a topic**. This may be as specific as you'd like or a broad one that you will break down later as your goals materialize. For your first mastermind group, it is recommended to pick a specific aspect of your life that you would like to begin making changes and improvements to.

The second step to creating a mastermind group is to **select individuals that align with your values and goals**. The purpose of this is so that mutual benefit occurs. You must not only be able to rely on your group members but they must be able to rely on you too. The size of mastermind groups varies and could have as few or many people as you'd like, a minimum of two or three for mutual benefit is recommended. Potential members should be people that have a similar drive and commitment so that you may all effectively work toward achieving your goals. Members should all boast varying skills so that the mastermind group is diverse, this will allow you to gain and share different perspectives toward a common goal.

Napoleon chose men whose qualities complemented his own so as to help him overcome his weaknesses. Henry Ford, too, integrated his energies with those of Thomas Edison, Harvey Firestone, Luther Burbank, and John Burroughs.

Everyone has shortcomings somewhere, which can be filled by other members of the mastermind group. One of the secrets of success is to be able to amplify one's personal power with the qualities of other people, that is, integrating one's mental energy with the intelligence, experience, knowledge and spiritual power of other complementary people.

Lastly, members should be problem solvers, this is necessary as people who enjoy solving problems have critical thinking skills that will lead to improvements in all aspects of your goals.

The third factor in creating a mastermind group is the **creation of rules.** This is to allow for respectful engagement and to ensure that feedback is not harmful or malicious. Now that you've completed these three steps the only thing left is to hold regular meetings for your group to interact and achieve.

Fig. 9: Mastermind groups facilitate for members to work toward a common goal.

Benefits of a Mastermind Group

There are many benefits to having and belonging to a mastermind group. The first **being mutual support and understanding**. Groups are often created with a specific goal in mind and if all members are in agreement with this goal they are then all working toward it. This will a certain subjectivity to be experienced and members will all be supporting each other in the achievement of the goal.

Mastermind groups while having specific goals consist of diverse members. This allows room for **different perspectives** that can be helpful when attempting to problem solve. These different views bring value as it illustrates another way in which something may be solved.

These groups **bring together resources**. That is, in addition to varying skill sets and perspectives, mastermind groups bring together people who have access to different types of resources that will assist in achieving goals more effectively and efficiently.

Moreover, the great strength is that **the group is worth more than the sum of the individuals**. The mere sum of individual contributions is less than the collective product of coordinated skills and efforts. The results that a mastermind can achieve will always be greater than what individual members could achieve individually.

An added benefit to mastermind groups is the **accountability** that the group facilitates. When working toward a common goal group members are able to hold each other to their agreed-upon goals and encourage each other to achieve excellence.

Mastermind groups are excellent in facilitating a safe space for bonds to form within a group. This allows **strong relationships** to form among group members. In a virtual setting with models of remote or smart working, the mastermind group will encourage team building and this will lead to better communication. It has the potential to make **work more productive** not only through problem-solving, brainstorming, or knowledge sharing but also through the skills that the mastermind group encourages. This includes communication and an open mind to diversity even though all members are working toward a common goal.

I encourage you to re-read this book several times very carefully. Each time you re-read it, you will find new concepts that you had missed before. Your awareness of group dynamics has changed. Now that you understand the principle of the master mind, you will understand even better the importance of collaboration and collaborative networks. The benefits of collaboration, are the benefits at the core of a mastermind group.

The Virtual Mastermind Group

Geographical location does not have to be a hindering factor against mastermind groups. As mentioned in previous chapters the business world has evolved to a point wherein technology has become a driving force toward innovation. This can be seen through remote working or a model of remote work known as smart working. Therefore, creating a virtual mastermind group is not only possible but will boost how a company works towards its objectives. Virtual mastermind groups will use the same factors of creating a mastermind group however, these groups will need a schedule that is adhered to so as to maximize the potential of the virtual mastermind group.

Advantages and Disadvantages of a Virtual Mastermind Group

The advantages of a virtual mastermind group are similar to the benefits of a mastermind group. However, using the internet creates a new pool of people with skills and perspectives that you might not have had access to. Thanks to the web you can create an ethereal and multiethnic group. Diversity causes learning to be more enriching and meaningful with more ideas from different perspectives thereby creating the best view of reality.

The disadvantages of a virtual mastermind group may manifest due to the poor planning and structure of the group. This includes but is not limited to, ineffective meetings, conflicting deadlines due to different time zones, and sometimes failure of tasks to be completed due to communication issues. It is also true that live relationships or meetings in person have a more harmonious flow due to a lack of physical boundaries and the ability of people to interact using emotion. This could indicate that in-person mastermind groups are more effective than virtual ones.

5. Virtual Teams

The social and technological changes our world is experiencing have drastically affected how people work. Faced with the opportunities and uncertainties that change brings, many businesses and companies have chosen to move their teams to the virtual world. This can be a daunting task especially when done haphazardly due to change. However, with the right mindset and knowledge of what virtual teams are and how to conduct them effectively your company has the potential to boost productivity.

Virtual teams are groups of people who may be located in different geographic areas, but who share common goals and objectives and work together through technology.

How to Create a Virtual Team

Creating teams that can collaborate effectively adds value to the company in terms of creativity, effectiveness, efficiency, new insights and breadth of vision.

Virtual teams are often a defining factor in a successful remote working model. Employees are in various geographical locations and work in different time zones. This can sometimes cause difficulties with scheduling and collaboration. Communication is not done in person and as such good communication and trusting your employees are essential in building a virtual team.

In order to create a virtual team, one must decide on their goals as well as the company's core values that they must emulate. There are various types of virtual teams depending on what your objectives are, so let's dive in; we will analyze ten types.

The first type of virtual team is called **networked teams** and this is wherein members with various skill sets that complement and cross each other are brought in. They can be in-house or external professionals (outsourcing). Members are experts in a particular field and come together to achieve a common goal. Members can also be removed once their role is complete and new ones brought in; there is no predetermined team.

This solution is widely used by consulting and technology companies. When there are specific needs that cannot be met by the company, a networked team is chosen. This option is capable of fulfilling any request from the clients. Even if the company does not specialize in the client's request, it is possible to find the specialized human resources that can fulfill that request.

The second team is **parallel teams**. They are usually made up of individuals working within the same organization. This is when a company forms a team with its employees to reach a particular goal. Therefore, team members are assigned tasks in addition to their primary tasks. Members do not often change and the team works toward improvement in processes that exist.

These members — from different functional areas, business units and locations — are tasked with addressing a problem, answering a market question and making recommendations for improving a process or system. All are driven to share their opinion and provide their knowledge to achieve predefined goals. They are highly focused on the task at hand and in most cases simply make recommendations.

This solution is often used by multinational companies that have employees with different backgrounds and knowledge spread across the globe. With parallel teams, they are able to bring together different skills and viewpoints, have multiple unique perspectives to the problem, and also encourage collaboration between different branches of the company.

They are also used by sales and marketing agencies, and research and development companies.

They are usually formed for a short period of time and members remain until the goal is accomplished. Once they complete their task, they can return to their primary duties, or take on subsequent tasks.

An example of parallel teams are *quality circles* (or quality control circles) that are formed to solve problems and improve the quality of services, processes, systems, or products. Members meet with management to discuss and propose improvement actions. They identify and analyze activities that need revision or improvement and solve problems.

Product development teams (or project development) are the third type of virtual team and rely on network collaboration. They are composed of experts from different parts of the world with the purpose of developing new products, information systems, organizational processes, delivering new technology systems or redesigning operational processes.

The effectiveness of this team is associated with the speed with which they are able to create and develop new products and services.

These teams often make up a company's research and

development department and help the business become more innovative and inventive. This requires a lot of experience and knowledge, and being able to bring together the best experienced product development talent from different parts of the world is a big plus. Assigning a task to a team of multidisciplinary individuals increases the level of creativity.

An example of this type is *cross-functional teams*, where members with different functional expertise work toward a common goal. Each member offers an alternative perspective to the problem and a potential solution to the task. Innovation is a key competitive advantage, and cross-functional teams foster innovation through a creative collaboration process.

The fourth type of virtual team a company can have is a **service team**, this relies on members being in different time zones so that the company can provide customer support 7 days a week, 24 hours a day.

Taking advantage of the different geographic locations allows you to support customers on an ongoing basis. For example, when the support team finishes their shift in one location, they start it on the other side of the world and continue their work.

With this system, there is never a break in communication. Providing customers with support outside of normal business hours increases customers appreciation for the company and the likelihood that they will recommend the company to others.

These virtual teams are commonly used for customer service and 24-hour support (customer service, after-sales service, and technical support).

The fifth type of team is **virtual management teams**, managers are in different geographical locations but are still able to collaborate on corporate upper-level decisions.

These teams primarily discuss corporate strategies and goals that their staff will then implement. They aim to make strategic decisions for the company even though members are often located far apart and in different countries and meet less frequently than other types of teams.

In addition to making important decisions, they oversee day-to-day operations, such as delegating tasks and monitoring employees. They often consist of managers from different divisions, and could be: Chairman, Chief Executive Officer (CEO), Chief Operating Officer (COO), Chief Financial Officer (CFO), Chief Marketing Officer (CMO), Chief Technology Officer (CTO), Chief Information Officer (CIO), Chief Knowledge Officer (CKO), Chief Security Officer (CSO), Chief risk officer (CRO), Chief Compliance Officer (CCO), Chief Sales Officer (CSO), Commercial Director, Hr Manager, R&D

Manager, Product Manager, Project Manager and Plant Manager.

An example of management teams are E*xecutive Management Teams*, which plan the various development processes and core business operations of the company as a whole, such as the development of financial matters and business plans. They consist of members at the top of the organization's hierarchy, such as the CEO and board of directors.

This type of team is often found in multinational corporations that have the management team dispersed across the nation or the world.

Sixth type. **Functional teams** are made up of people from the same department or area and usually perform a single, well-defined activity. Members have well-defined roles and collaborate on regular and ongoing activities. They perform precisely functional activities, so they can be found in any type of company. These teams often work together over a long period of time.

One example is *production teams*, which consist of members with a well-defined role who come together to perform regular, ongoing tasks. They usually work independently, and their combined efforts produce the end result.

Seventh type. **Action teams** are formed to respond to

immediate problems and are very short duration. They are made up of experts who come together in times of emergency or extraordinary situations to quickly find an immediate solution to a problem. Once the issue is resolved, the team is disbanded.

They are similar to parallel teams, but the key difference is that parallel teams make recommendations for improvements, while action teams have the ability to take action to implement solutions.

They can be found in any organization regardless of type or industry. They are widely used by engineering companies.

We can also take the example of *task forces* (an emergency response unit), which are a group of experts, from different business sectors and with different professional experience, who come together to develop ideas, create new opportunities or solve a specific problem. These teams are tasked with addressing particular situations.

The expression task force has its origin in the military lexicon, but is now also used in various political and work contexts.

Team outsourcing is another type of team, used by those who prefer to delegate particular tasks to external entities. Outsourcing acts as an emergency exit which is offered by the human resources (HR) department to the executives having trouble in competitive environment (Ates, 2013).

Cost reduction, support of companies' growth strategies, competitive pressure, and access to qualified personnel for example, are strategic drivers for offshoring (Peeters & Lewin, 2006).

Many companies outsource tasks to other countries, where the cost of getting the work done is lower, trying to lower costs without significantly sacrificing quality. Thus, a collaboration is established between internal company teams and external teams.

This can be a beneficial solution, but there are also many issues that need to be addressed. There are many businesses that choose the wrong companies and end up with many failed projects.

Often results are different from what one would like because the team starts working on the project without a full understanding of the project specifications. This is also due to poor communication due to language barriers.

Late deliveries are another problem. These teams work on multiple projects for many clients and may not spend enough time on your project. Finally there can be a lack of confidentiality, these teams can violate the NDA (non-disclosure agreement) and steal trade secrets.

Fig. 10: The technology used for virtual team collaboration

Key factors in outsourcing success are the decision process, partners, contract and partnership quality. The choice of outsourcing partnership should be based on a social, rather than an economic, perspective. Partnership quality is formed by factors such as trust, business understanding, benefit/risk share, conflict and commitment (Ates, 2013); and is positively influenced by factors such as participation, communication, information sharing, and top management support, and negatively affected by age of relationship and mutual dependency (Lee & Kim, 1999).

An example of such teams are *offshore ISD teams* (information systems development teams). Offshore ISD is commonly used for software development. More and more companies are outsourcing these tasks to offshore companies where the skill set is great and doesn't push the budget out of bounds.

You need to be very careful, though. Contemporary offshore information system development outsourcing is becoming even more complex. Outsourcing partner has begun "re-outsourcing" components of their projects to other outsourcing companies to minimize cost and gain efficiencies (Maduka Nuwangi et al., 2014). This means that some of the problems you may experience can be amplified.

Another type are **global virtual teams** (GVT). They can be defined as a group of people who work on interdependent tasks guided by a common purpose across space, time and organizational boundaries with technology-supported communication substantially more than face-to-face meetings (adapted from Maznevski & Chudoba, 2000) and also as a group of workers, formally recognized by the organization as a team, with members from different countries who are collectively accountable for outputs across locations, and who utilize technology to some degree to accomplish their work (Gibson & Grushina, 2021).

Finally, you may also find **hybrid teams** where some people work in the office and others work remotely. This could be a great solution for sales companies where salespeople work in different geographic areas close to their customers, as well as increasing conversion rates, they can offer better customer service and after-sales support.

There are more types of virtual teams but as expanded on above, only when the company goals and values are clearly defined can a virtual team be formed.

Advantages and Disadvantages of Virtual Teams

The advantages of virtual teams are similar to those of remote working and include but are not limited to, flexibility, decreased office costs, an increase in productivity, a larger pool of skills and knowledge to choose from, and lastly the ability of a company to have twenty-four-hour operations with teams working virtually in different time zones.

The disadvantages of virtual teams are that there could be technological failures that would hinder work. Virtual teams rely on the internet and other forms of technology for their work to be successful when these systems go down then work cannot be completed. Another issue virtual teams could run into is poor communication and management. Without strong leaders, virtual teams will not have the direction or motivation to complete tasks and stay on until objectives are completed. Tips on how to avoid these are discussed below.

How to Effectively Manage and Optimize Performance of a Virtual Team

Teams need to institute better organizational processes and protocols for how work and communication about work happens.

Communication can be hindered as people are not speaking face-to-face. To ensure that management is able to still get work done and achieve company objectives adaptation is necessary. To better manage your team your employees must be given **adequate technology** so that they are able to connect with each other and management. This will allow a harmonious and uninterrupted workflow. The best technology is not limited to the hardware, for example, laptops, tablets, or smartphones, but also the software that employees have access to. Giving your employees the best possible resources will boost their ability to work remotely and ensure that they are producing quality work.

The second way to effectively manage a virtual team is by **planning your tasks** and having a schedule for how they are to be completed. It is necessary to clearly communicate realistic goals and deadlines for work to be effectively and efficiently done. In order to optimize the virtual team's performance it is necessary for management to delegate tasks; this means that **every role must be clearly laid out** so that employees understand what is expected of them. Everyone needs to know what to do, how to do it, and when to do it. This holds people accountable and the team will be able to work more efficiently. Management should **create smaller tasks** that form part of the bigger picture so that work is manageable and within realistic parameters for completion. This will allow for work to be done in a timely fashion and be of a high quality.

Managers should also **keep track** of those who are producing great work. When working virtually it is easy for achievements to go unnoticed. A trait of good leadership is the ability of managers to recognize what members are bringing to the team and when to thank individuals as well as the team. It is also important for managers to **maintain a work/life balance** for their employees and to encourage them to unplug especially when goals are being met. Well-rested employees will produce better work in the hours that they do have available.

In this vein, a change of pace is necessary in terms of cultural change, in order to support workers and organizations to address the challenges posed by this relatively new approach, delimiting the borders between work and nonwork and managing the expectation of constant availability and reachability, which are typical of Italian organizations (Molino et al. 2020).

Increase Collaboration Skills

We've seen above how important collaboration is, but it doesn't happen immediately between team members. It takes time and effort to get to know teammates and establish a good working relationship. There are four determining factors that can help and foster collaboration among members: *communication skills*, *listening skills*, *emotional intelligence*, and *respect for diversity*.

Developing good **communication skills** is a key factor in building good relationships and rapport. Any type of communication brings us into relationship with others, so it is very important to be careful how we communicate also because how we communicate affects who we become. Thinking before you speak, choosing your words carefully and expressing your opinions respectfully is a good start.

In order to communicate effectively, it is necessary to

develop good **listening skills**, which are also essential for good collaboration. As the ancient Greek philosopher Zeno of Citium taught us, the reason why we have two ears and only one mouth is that we may listen more and talk less. A few centuries later, Plutarch also reiterated that nature has given each of us two ears and one tongue because we ought to do less talking than listening.

Listening also means having respect for the interlocutor. We must not use *passive listening*, which is often used to discourage the speaker, nor *selective listening*, which is usually used to counterattack, but *active listening*: the ability to give full attention to our interlocutor (pay full attention to both verbal and non-verbal communication).

> "When something is poured, people tilt and rotate the vessels so that the operation is successful and there is no dispersion, while when they listen they do not learn to offer themselves to the speaker and to follow carefully, so that no useful affirmation escapes them."
>
> Plutarch

Active listening helps us to truly understand the other person and fully comprehend the messages being communicated, helps us to establish solid, trusting relationships, and improves knowledge transfer. By listening we learn!

Finally, the ability to listen reduces tensions between members because those who are listened to lower their defenses and reduce their aggression.

The third factor is **emotional intelligence**; there are many definitions and they relate to the ability to recognize, use, understand and consciously manage one's own emotions and those of others. I disagree, though. We are not robots that can control and manage our emotions, but we can control and manage our reactions in front of an emotion.

Emotional intelligence is a skill that helps us perceive, understand and manage our own reactions and those of others when the mind offers us an emotion in response to an experience we are having.[10]

[10]. I would like to make some clarifications. We are not our mind, we are a primordial consciousness. The ontological nature of the human being is spiritual. We are endowed with a very sophisticated on-board instrument that is our mind that allows us to interact in the physical world.

Our mind allows us to connect to matter in the material world and thus allows this dimensional connection between our spiritual dimension and the physical dimension of the material world.

When we have an experience, the mind offers us an emotion. Our emotions are offered to us by our mind as a response to the experience we are having. We can react with a reactive method (undergo the "provocation") or with a reflective method: act as an external observer, observe what is happening around us both on an environmental and psychic level, become aware of the here and now, distance ourselves from emotional conditioning, depower emotional charges and contemplate.

We do not control or manage emotions, but rather reactions.

This skill is useful for understanding how other team members feel and understanding when they need help and support. This improves collaboration.

The fourth factor is **respect for diversity**. Collaboration thrives in an environment that respects diversity, avoids discrimination, and is sensitive to the ethnic and religious backgrounds of other team members.

Effective Habits for Teams

There are some really effective habits that can elevate team performance. The first is to **invest time in getting to know each other** to develop the capacity for human connection. Once the team is created, each member should familiarize themselves with each other and understand their personal backgrounds, skills, limitations and strengths; get in touch with their experiences, knowledge and expertise. It will be helpful to talk about things in life to connect on a human level, meet physically to have fun, play games and eat something together.

The second is to **be success-oriented.** Etymologically, the word "*success*" comes from the Latin word "succedĕre" meaning "*to go up*" or "*to follow*". Dictionaries define success with the meaning of "*to succeed well*" or "*to obtain a desired object or purpose*".

From this perspective, there is no single objective measure of success. It has to do with the ability to achieve goals. Essentially, "*being successful*" has to do with developing the skills and resources necessary to achieve the results you desire.

The goals have several levels:

- *Environmental Level: producing or owning something*

- *Behavioral Level: doing something you want to do or overcoming a physical challenge*

- *Ability Level: developing or applying a particular skill*

- *Beliefs and Values Level: acting or living according to your principles and philosophy*

- *Identity Level: becoming a certain type of person or fulfilling your calling*

- *Vision and Purpose Level: to make a contribution or*

"create a world where people want to belong".

So it is possible to be simultaneously successful at different levels, or to be successful at one level but not at others.

Success orientation leads to developing another habit: **constantly looking for ways to improve**. This can be sharing best practices, having a desire to innovate, and wanting to implement new ideas to improve the business. Meet regularly to talk about what's working and what's not. Teams should spend time asking questions like "*What can we improve?*" or "*How can we improve?*" The nature of life is to aspire to more and more life; our human nature is to desire a better, happier, richer, and more abundant life. To be inspired to grow, rise and advance is to honor life.

Another habit is having legendary **mental clarity** about how to carry out the workday: being focused only on what is really important; daily tasks should not be random, but rather specific action steps that help move you closer to a goal; knowing exactly what to do, how to do it, and when to do it. Clarity of mind helps keep purpose in the forefront and have a clear sense of the company's mission.

The habit of **celebrating successes** is another great habit. Before thinking about the next goal, it's important to celebrate. Once we get what we want, it's important to enjoy it. Celebrating successes gets us energized and we will be more motivated to achieve our next goals.

It is a good habit to also stop and reflect on the elements that allowed us to reach that goal, this helps us become more aware of our strength and increases our self-confidence.

Plan a nice group dinner, trip, memorable experience of any kind or give yourself a gift. Reward yourself! Share the happiness with the people around you. After the effort comes the reward. You must acknowledge to yourself what you have done, and express your gratitude; it will help open more doors to welcome more positive events.

But the most important thing is not to wait until we reach a certain goal to be happy. No matter where we go and what we achieve, the key is to enjoy the journey; to enjoy every single moment of this amazing journey called life.

Finally, the habit of **being highly productive**. Avoid information overload, multitasking, and constant interruptions. Marry the principle of single-handing and apply all the productivity strategies expressed above.

Virtues of Virtual Teams

Teams should have virtues – constant dispositions of mind

to do good that drive members to strive for high ends – to live and work righteously and in harmony.

To be aware of what it means to be a member of a team, to be reliable and take responsibility; to develop strength and temperance so as not to lose balance in virtual environments; to avoid insults; not to invade spaces with spam; develop the capacity for selective attention so as not to be taken away; develop the ability to filter information by selecting it from the correct sources without conflicts of interest; do not give in to the conformism of social networks, so as not to lose one's identity and exalt one's uniqueness; maintain general interest in projects; have a dialogue to set clear objectives, define roles and responsibilities in advance; compromise for the best interest of the group; think and reflect before acting; do not stop at appearances; increase the critical capacity towards what surrounds us; get out of egocentrism to allow a group spirit in which interactions become meaningful.

Tips on Virtual Teams

Communication is essential when working with and in a virtual team. You need to provide clear instructions and have adequate technological support.

Using all available communication tools ensures that team

members have any way possible to contact management. Additionally, communication tools and scheduling will allow for **more effective meeting preparation.**

Meetings are very important, but they can become a waste of time. So here are a few tips to increase their efficiency and effectiveness:

- *Don't schedule a meeting during highly productive hours.*

- *The meeting must have a start and end time, a clear agenda, and a clearly defined end goal.*

- *Start the meeting with an element of breaking: 1 minute of silence.*

- *The conduct of the meeting must be in monofocus and monotasking mode: there is only the meeting, no distractions, maximum concentration, staying in the present moment.*

- *Be polite and have respect for the meeting: remove smartphones and tablets from your field of vision; if you can't turn them off because you're addicted to them, at least turn off notifications.*

- *Not attending meetings that do not serve the company's growth and project development.*

Scheduling meetings that are not too frequent but within a realistic schedule will allow employees to complete tasks and have enough information to engage with management. This will lead to better planning to reach company objectives.

A good **leadership** style is essential in running a virtual team. Choosing leaders is sometimes necessary to set an example, foster open lines of communication, and facilitate meetings and tasks. A true leader will be able to carefully select people who they know will drive the company objectives and inspire others to share their skills and knowledge. Strong leaders will also be able to motivate their teams and encourage each member in their strengths so that an overall goal may be met. Team members will be more inclined to engage and this too will result in a better quality project.

Identifying and maximizing **the strengths** of each team member is very important as each person will bring something valuable to the project. Members need to do fewer administrative tasks and focus on what they are good at. This results in better results and satisfaction in the long-term.

Establishing **Extreme Productivity Day** is a treat, where all team members keep their phones off and don't check email. People know they won't be looked for and won't look for others so they don't give and receive interruptions.

Having **interdependent goals** will foster collaboration because members will need each other to succeed.

Make sure there is a good **range of skills** among the members. We've already addressed that a team with a diverse set of skills, expertise, experience, and perspectives will be stronger.

Membership in a team must be stable over time; the team does not develop its full potential when people are constantly joining and leaving.

With a virtual team, there are often members who are part of the team that works from international locations. This leads to the **interaction of different types of culture** especially in terms of business practices. Leaders and members should keep an open mind and be willing to understand and compromise. This will allow the strong foundation of trust to build as well as forge strong, lasting relationships.

Promoting **mutual listening** and creating a team of attentive listeners will be another added value.

A good virtual team does not have too many members and rather focuses on solid communication, the ability to work independently, and for team members to have good emotional intelligence. These factors are what will allow a team to work effectively and efficiently even though they are not working face-to-face.

Conclusion

This guide has explained in-depth the concepts of remote and smart working, as well as collaborative networks, mastermind groups and how to create virtual teams using mastermind principles. The advantages and disadvantages of each topic have created a clear picture of how you should plan the creation of your teams using models of remote or smart work.

The world is ever-changing and that is true for the business world as well. The changes and experiences that the world has gone through in the last years has vastly shifted the way we look at work and the way we think about working and solving problems. Remote work, while not a new concept, has gained popularity and it is during this time that companies should begin shifting their ideas around remote working models. They have the potential to produce some of the best quality work while affording employees flexibility with regards to location, hours, and often even the type of work available.

The Limits Are Only in Your Mind

Use everything you have learned in this book to bring about innovation in your company. From new international projects to international collaborations you now have the knowledge to create virtual companies that serve an even bigger market, expanding your company's reach. Broaden your market and business with an improved knowledge base that you will achieve through mastermind groups, boasting members from all over the world. Understanding the importance of groups and implementing this in your company will prove to be a priceless asset.

Groups are able to enhance the strengths of individuals, allowing you to make the most of your skills and those of others. Groups provide an opportunity to find collaborators who bring solutions, people who are committed to understanding your goals. It will allow you to engage with people of varying skill sets and intelligence levels, people who bring solutions. You will interact with a diversity that has lived different experiences and who have the potential to bring better results.

The limits are only in your mind.

I'm sitting here in my chair observing a black swan that is white. Perturbation is inevitable. Technology disruption is inevitable. You'll need to dust off your spade, cooperate with the ground, cooperate with plants and animals. If it is true that we are all interconnected, you will meet me on this page at the appropriate time.

Lucky is the person, who will learn to master the power of the mastermind.

Photo Credits

Fig. 1: *Photo by Marvin Meyer* on Unsplash.com. https://unsplash.com/photos/SYTO3xs06fU

Fig. 2: *Photo by Magnet.me* on Unsplash.com. https://unsplash.com/photos/LDcC7aCWVlo

Fig. 3: *Photo by Daria Mamont* on Unsplash.com. https://unsplash.com/photos/qzdHPRTnawg

Fig. 4: *Photo by LinkedIn Sales Solutions* on Unsplash.com. https://unsplash.com/photos/Be5aVKFv9ho

Fig. 5: *Photo by Jason Goodman* on Unsplash.com. https://unsplash.com/photos/Oalh2MojUuk

Fig. 6: *Photo by LinkedIn Sales Solutions* on Unsplash.com. https://unsplash.com/photos/FCr_Oglkth0

Fig. 7: "Body, Biofield and Mental Electric Field." by Zeloni Magelli

Fig. 8: *Photo by Brooke Cagle* on Unsplash.com. https://unsplash.com/photos/g1Kr4Ozfoac

Fig. 9: *Photo by Jed Villejo* on Unsplash.com. https://unsplash.com/photos/bEcC0nyIp2g

Fig. 10: *Photo by Gabriel Benois* on Unsplash.com. https://unsplash.com/photos/qnWPjzewewA

Bibliographical References

American Chemical Society (2016). *Selecting the right house plant could improve indoor air (animation).* Philadelphia, Aug. 24, 2016 Retrivied from https://www.acs.org/content/acs/en/pressroom/newsreleases/2016/august/selecting-the-right-house-plant-could-improve-indoor-air-animation.html

Afsarmanesh, H., Camarinha-Matos, L. M., (2005). A Framework for Management of Virtual Organization Breeding Environments. In: Collaborative Networks and their Breeding Environments, Springer, pp. 35-48, Valencia, Spain, 26-28 Sept 2005.

Akbar, F., et al. (2019). *Email Makes You Sweat: Examining Email Interruptions and Stress Using Thermal Imaging.* Proceedings of the 2019 CHI Conference on Human Factors in Computing Systems. DOI:10.1145/3290605.3300898

Angulo, P., S., De Benito, J., J., Araúzo, J. A., (n.d.). *An Agent-Based Framework for Selection of Partners in Dynamic Virtual Enterprises.* Framed inside the Project DPI2001-1903, financed by the Spain Ministry of Science and Technology.

Armstrong, M. J. (2017). Improving email strategies to target stress and productivity in clinical practice. *Neurology Clinical Practice.* 2017 Dec; 7(6): 512–517. DOI:10.1212/CPJ.0000000000000395

Ates, M. Fikret. (2013). The Effect of Partnership Quality on Outsourcing Success in Human Resources Functions. *International Journal of Academic Research in Business and Social Sciences*. 3. 10.6007/IJARBSS/v3-i12/487.

Babauta, L. (2009) *The Power of LESS: The 6 Essential Productivity Principles That Will Change Your Life.* Hay House.

Berkley, University of Califorinia. (2021). *When everyone works remotely, communication and collaboration suffer, study finds.* Phys.org. https://phys.org/news/2021-09-remotely-collaboration.html

Bernardi, L. (2018). *Biorisonanza quantistica e riequilibrio energetico*. Progetto Benessere Completo. Retrivied from https://www.progettobenesserecompleto.it/articoli/biorisonanza-quantistica-e-riequilibrio-energetico

Bayern, M. (2019). *Why remote work has grown by 159% since 2005* https://www.techrepublic.com/article/why-remote-work-has-grown-by-159-since-2005/

Bondanini, G., Giorgi, G., Ariza-Montes, A., Vega-Muñoz, A., & Andreucci-Annunziata, P. (2020). Technostress Dark Side of Technology in the Workplace: A Scientometric Analysis. *International journal of environmental research and public health*, *17*(21), 8013. https://doi.org/10.3390/ijerph17218013

Bradberry, T. (n.d.). *Multitasking Damages Your Brain and Your Career, New Studies Suggest..* TalentSmart EQ. Retrieved July 7, 2019, from https://www.talentsmart.com/articles/Multitasking-Damages-Your-Brain-and-Your-Career,-New-Studies-Suggest-2102500909-p-1.html

Bradt, S. (2010). *Wandering mind not a happy mind.* The Harvard Gazzette https://news.harvard.edu/gazette/story/2010/11/wandering-mind-not-a-happy-mind/

Brod C., (1984). Technostress: The Human Cost of the Computer Revolution. Addison-Wesley; Reading, MA, USA: 1984.

Camarinha-Matos, L. M., (2009). Collaborative Networks Contribution to Sustainable Development. In: Proceedings of SWIIS 2009 – *IFAC Workshop on Supplementary Ways for Improving International Stability (invited)*, Bucharest, Romania, 28-30 Oct 2009. ID 10.3182/20091028-3-RO-4007.00020.

Camarinha-Matos, L. M., (2004). Virtual Enterprises and Collaborative Networks: IFIP 18th World Computer Congress TC5/WG5.5 — 5th Working Conference on Virtual Enterprises 22–27 August 2004 Toulouse, France. Springer.

Camarinha-Matos, L. M., & Afsarmanesh, H., (2005). Collaborative Networks: A New Scientific Discipline. Journal of Intelligent Manufacturing 16, 439-452.

Camarinha-Matos, L. M., & Afsarmanesh, H., (n.d.). Collaborative Networks. *IFIP International Federation for Information Processing*, 26–40. https://doi.org/10.1007/0-387-34403-9_4

Camarinha-Matos, L. M., Benaben, F., Picard, W. (2015). Risks and Resilience of Collaborative Networks: 16th IFIP WG 5.5 Working Conference on Virtual Enterprises, PRO-VE 2015, Albi, France, October 5-7, 2015, Proceedings. Springer.

Carciofi, A. (2017). Digital Detox: Focus & Produttività per il manager nell'era delle distrazioni digitali. Milano, Hoelpi.

Centro di Medicina Biologica, (2019). *Biorisonanza quantistica.* Centro di Medicina Biologica. Retrieved from https://www.centrodimedicinabiologica.it/terapie/medicina-quantistica-biorisonanza/

Civil Service College. (2018). *Understanding the differences between teamwork and collaboration.* Civil Service College. https://www.civilservicecollege.org.uk/news-understanding-the-differences-between-teamwork-and-collaboration-203

Clark, M. A., Smith, R. W., Haynes, N. J. (2020). The Multidimensional Workaholism Scale: linking the conceptualization and measurement of workaholism. *Journal of Applied Psychology*, 105(11), 1281. https://doi.org/10.1037/apl0000484

Di Stefano, G. & Gaudiino, M. (2019) Workaholism and work engagement: how are they similar? How are they different? A systematic review and meta-analysis, *European Journal of Work and Organizational Psychology,* 28:3, 329-347, DOI: 10.1080/1359432X.2019.1590337

Dean, K. L. (2013). *Alternative and Complementary Therapies.* Jun 2003.142-145.http://doi.org/10.1089/107628003322017396

Dépincé, P., Chablat, D., Woelk, P-O. (2004). Virtual Manufacturing: Tools for improving Design and Production. *CIRP International Design Seminar*, 2004, Caire, Egypt. pp.1-12.

Fels, D. (2018). The Double-Aspect of Life. *Biology*, 7(2), 28. doi:10.3390/biology7020028

Formisano, M. (2016). *Produttività 300%: Triplica i risultati e Goditi la vita.* Torino, Uno Editori

Franssila, H., Okkonen, J.M., & Savolainen, R. (2014). Email intensity, productivity and control in the knowledge worker's performance on the desktop. *MindTrek*.

Galeano Sánchez, N., G., Guerra Zubiaga, D., A., Irigoyen González, J., A., Molina, A. (n.d.). *Virtual Breeding Environment: A First Approach to Understand Working and Sharing Principles* Centre for Integrated Manufacturing Systems, Eugenio Garza Sada 2501, 64849 Monterrey, Mexico

Gibson, C. B., Grushina, S. V. (2021). "A Tale of Two Teams: Next Generation Strategies for Increasing the Effectiveness of Global Virtual Teams". *Organizational Dynamics*. Virtual Teams. 50 (1): 100823. doi:10.1016/j.orgdyn.2020.100823. ISSN 0090-2616.

Goleman, D. (2014). *Focus. The Hidden Driver of Ecellence* (trad. it. *Focus: come mantenersi concentrati nell'era della distrazione.* Best BUR, 2016)

Griffin, L. (2019). Network Switching: Definition & Types. *Study.com,* 29 October 2019. Retrieved from https://study.com/academy/lesson/network-switching-definition-types.html.

Griffiths, M. D., Demetrovics, Z., Atroszko, P. A. (2018). Ten myths about work addiction. *Journal of Behavioral Addictions*, 7 (4), 845–857. https://doi.org/10.155 /2006.7.2018.05

Hyken, S. (2021). *The Impact Of The Remote Workforce*. Forbes. https://www.forbes.com/sites/shephyken/2021/02/28/the-impact-of-the-virtual-work-from-home-workforce/.

Jackson, DJ. (2011) '*What is an Innovation Ecosystem?*' National Science Foundation, Arlington, VA

Jones, Timothy T. (2015). *Monitoring Volatile Organic Compounds Removal by Indoor Plants*. 2015 SUNY Undergraduate Research Conference.

Kafatos, M. C., Chevalier, G., Chopra, D., Hubacher, J., Kak, S., & Theise, N. D. (2015). Biofield Science: Current Physics Perspectives. *Global advances in health and medicine*, 4(Suppl), 25–34. https://doi.org/10.7453/gahmj.2015.011.suppl

Kekatos, M. (2021). *Fully remote workers spend 25% less time collaborating, have fewer real-time conversations and decrease hours spent in meetings by 5%, study of Microsoft employees finds*. Dailymail.Com https://www.dailymail.co.uk/health/article-9973963/Fully-remote-workers-spend-25-time-collaborating-fewer-real-time-conversations.html

Keller, G. and Papasan, J. (2018). Il Segreto nella vita è scegliere UNA COSA SOLA su cui concentrarsi per ottenere risultati eccezionali. TEA

Koschtial, C. (2021). Understanding e-Science—What Is It About? DOI:10.1007/978-3-030-66262-2_1 In book: e-Science, Open, Social and Virtual Technology for Research Collaboration (pp.1-9)

Kürümlüoglu, M., Nostdal, R., & Karvonen, I. (2005). Base concepts. In L. M. Camarinha-Matos, H. Afsarmanesh, & M. Ollus (Eds.), *Virtual Organizations: Systems and Practies* (pp. 11-28). Springer.

Lee, Jae-Nam & Kim, Young-Gul (1999) Effect of Partnership Quality on IS Outsourcing Success: Conceptual Framework and Empirical Validation, Journal of Management Information Systems, 15:4, 29-61, DOI: 10.1080/07421222.1999.11518221

Levin, D., Z., Walter, J., Appleyard, M., M. (2011). *Trusted Network-Bridging Ties: A Dyadic Approach to the Brokerage-Closure Dilemma.* http://www.levin.rutgers.edu/research/trusted-bridging-ties-paper.pdf

Lifegate, (2009). *Medicina quantistica: cos'è la cura quantica e come funziona.* Lifegate. Retrieved from https://www.lifegate.it/medicina_quantistica_come_cura

Longqi Yang, David Holtz, Sonia Jaffe, Siddharth Suri, Shilpi Sinha, Jeffrey Weston, Connor Joyce, Neha Shah, Kevin Sherman, Brent Hecht & Jaime Teevan. (2021). The effects of remote work on collaboration among information workers, *Nature Human Behaviour* (2021). DOI: 10.1038/s41562-021-01196-4

Lowrie, Lisa M. (2019). *Exploring the relationships of Email Overload, Stress and Burnout in Social Workers Social Work Doctoral Dissertations.* 9. https://research.library.kutztown.edu/socialworkdissertations/9

Maduka Nuwangi, S., Sedera, D., C. Srivastava, S. and Murphy, G. (2014), "Intra-organizational information asymmetry in offshore ISD outsourcing", *VINE*, Vol. 44 No. 1, pp. 94-120. https://doi.org/10.1108/VINE-04-2013-0023

Mark, G., Iqbal, S. T., Czerwinski, M., Johns, P., Sano, A., Lutchyn, Y. (2016). *Email Duration, Batching and Self-interruption: Patterns of Email Use on Productivity and Stress.* Proceedings of the 2016 CHI Conference on Human Factors in Computing Systems. DOI:10.1145/2858036.2858262

Martínez-Córcoles M., Teichmann M., Murdvee M. (2017). Assessing technophobia and technophilia: Development and validation of a questionnaire. *Technol. Soc.* 2017;51:183–188. doi: 10.1016/j.techsoc.2017.09.007.

Maznevski, M. L. & Chudoba, K. M. (2000). Bridging space over time: Global virtual team dynamics and effectiveness. *Organization Science*, 11(5), 473–492. https://doi.org/10.1287/orsc.11.5.473.15200

McKusick, E. D. (2014). *Tuning the Human Biofield: Healing with Vibrational Sound Therapy.* Healing Arts Press. Rochester, Vermont.

Miltz, A. (2020). *Remote work frequency before/after COVID-19 2020.* Statista. https://www.statista.com/statistics/1122987/change-in-remote-work-trends-after-covid-in-usa/

Molino, M., Ingusci, E., Signore, F., Manuti, A., Giancaspro, M. L., Russo, V., Zito, M., Cortese, C. G. (2020). Wellbeing Costs of Technology Use during Covid-19 Remote Working: An Investigation Using the Italian Translation of the Technostress Creators Scale. *Sustainability*. 12(15):5911 DOI:10.3390/su12155911

Morkevičiūtė, M. & Endriulaitiene, A. (2021). *Workaholism and Work Addiction: The Differeces in Motivational factors*. October 2021. DOI:10.15388/Soctyr.44.2.6

Muehsam, D., Chevalier, G., Barsotti, T., & Gurfein, B. T. (2015). An Overview of Biofield Devices. *Global advances in health and medicine*, 4(Suppl), 42–51. https://doi.org/10.7453/gahmj.2015.022.suppl

Newport, C. (2021). *A World Without Email: Reimagining Work in an Age of Communication Overload.* USA: Portfolio, Penguin.

Niu, D. (2021). *New Hires Suffering in Silence: Two Key Ingredients Missing from Remote Onboarding Programs.* TINYpulse. https://www.tinypulse.com/blog/new-hires-suffering-in-silence-wfh-remote-onboarding

Oates, W.E. (1971). *Confessions of a workaholic: The facts about work addiction.* New York: World.

Ouzounis, E. K. (2001). *An Agent-Based Platform for the Management of Dynamic Virtual Enterprises.* Dissertation von der Fakultät Elektrotechnik und Informatik der Technischen. Universität Berlin.

Peeters, C. & Lewin, A. (2006). *Offshoring administrative and technical work: business hype or the onset of fundamental strategic and organizational transformation?.* ULB - Universite Libre de Bruxelles, ULB Institutional Repository.

PMI.it, (2021). *Ufficio, casa o smart working? Le preferenze degli italiani.* https://www.pmi.it/economia/lavoro/350992/home-o-smart-working-le-preferenze-degli-italiani.html

Popp, F. A., & Beloussov, L. V. (Eds.). (2013). *Integrative biophysics: biophotonics.* Springer Science & Business Media.

Prossack, A. (2021). *5 Statistics Employers Need To Know About The Remote Workforce.* Forbes. https://www.forbes.com/sites/ashiraprossack1/2021/02/10/5-statistics-employers-need-to-know-about-the-remote-workforce/?sh=492b3df0655d

Reynolds, B. W. (n.d.). *The Mental Health Benefits of Remote and Flexible Work.* Mental Health America.

https://mhanational.org/blog/mental-health-benefits-remote-and-flexible-work

Ribeiro, L., Barata, J. (2006). *New Shop Floor Control Approaches for Virtual Enterprises.* Enterprise and Work Innovation Studies, No. 2, 2006 IET, Monte de Caparica, Portugal

Roe, D., (2021). *Is Remote Working Really Impeding Collaboration and Communication?.* Reworked. https://www.reworked.co/digital-workplace/is-remote-working-really-impeding-collaboration-and-communication/

Rubik, B., Muehsam, D., Hammerschlag, R., & Jain, S. (2015). Biofield Science and Healing: History, Terminology, and Concepts. *Global advances in health and medicine*, *4*(Suppl), 8–14. https://doi.org/10.7453/gahmj.2015.038.suppl

Salanova M., Llorens S., Ventura M. (2014). *Technostress: The dark side of technologies.* In: Korunka C., Hoonakker P., editors. The impact of ICT on Quality of Working Life. Springer; Dordrecht, The Netherlands: pp. 87–103.

Scholkmann, F., Fels, D., & Cifra, M. (2013). Non-chemical and non-contact cell-to-cell communication: a short review. *American journal of translational research*, *5*(6), 586–593.

Scholten, V., Omta, O., Kemp, R., Elfring, T. (2015). Bridging ties and the role of research and start-up experience on the early growth of Dutch academic spin-offs. *Technovation.* Volumes 45–46, November–December 2015, Pages 40-51

Simon, B. (2017). *Collaboration Networks: Bringing Together a Team to Accomplish Your Projects.* Smartsheet https://www.smartsheet.com/collaboration-networks

Tarafdar, M.; Tu, Q.; Ragu-Nathan, T.S. (2010). Impact of technostress on end-user satisfaction and performance. *J. Manag. Inf. Syst.* 2010, 27, 303–334.

Toyoda, M., Yokota, Y., Barnes, M., & Kaneko, M. (2020). Potential of a Small Indoor Plant on the Desk for Reducing Office Workers' Stress. *Horttechnology*, 30, 55-63.

Tracy, B. (2013). *Time Management*. Amacom. (trad. it *Gestione del Tempo*. Milano, Gribaudi, 2015)

Weil, M.M.; Rosen, L.D. (1997). *Technostress: Coping with Technology @Work @Home @Play*; Wiley: New York NY, USA, 1997.

Wolverton, B. B., Nelson M. (2020). "Using plants and soil microbes to purify indoor air: lessons from NASA and Biosphere 2 experiments", *Field Actions Science Reports* [Online], Special Issue 21 | 2020, Online since 24 February 2020, connection on 09 January 2021. URL: http://journals.openedition.org/factsreports/6092

Wolverton, B. C., Johnson, A., Bounds, K. (1989). *Interior Landscape Plants for Indoor Air Pollution Abatement.* NASA. September 15, 1989. https://ntrs.nasa.gov/api/citations/19930073077/downloads/19930073077.pdf

Yassa, Morcous M., Hassan, Hesham A., Omara, Fatma A. (2014). Utilizing CommonKADS as Problem-Solving and Decision-Making for Supporting Dynamic Virtual Organization Creation. IAES *International Journal of Artificial Intelligence* (IJ-AI) Vol. 3, No. 1, March 2014, pp. 1~6 ISSN: 2252-8938

Zeloni Magelli, E. (2020). *Miglioramento della Memoria: Il Libro sulla Memoria per Incrementare la Potenza Cerebrale - Cibo e Sane Abitudini per il Cervello per Aumentare la Memoria, Ricordare di Più e Dimenticare di Meno.* Edoardo Zeloni Magelli

www.ingramcontent.com/pod-product-compliance
Lightning Source LLC
LaVergne TN
LVHW011834060526
838200LV00053B/4019